THE
ART OF WORSHIP

THE
ART OF WORSHIP

AL KINRADE

authorHOUSE®

AuthorHouse™
1663 Liberty Drive
Bloomington, IN 47403
www.authorhouse.com
Phone: 1-800-839-8640

Published by AuthorHouse   08/15/2012

ISBN: 978-1-4685-7211-7 (sc)
ISBN: 978-1-4685-7212-4 (e)

Library of Congress Control Number: 2012905625

Contents

"THE ART OF WORSHIP"
AND SERVICE
NOTATION

Special notation: I will not dignify the proper name of satan, or the pronouns (he, him, his) when referring to satan, by capitalizing the first letter. This is done throughout! Also, Scripture references used herein are by no means exhaustive; but, are merely the foundation which hopefully support my comments. Also, there are duplications or repeats at certain points that are needed as reminders when dealing with a specific issue. As a professor in seminary constantly reminded us, "Repetition is the key to remembering."

Almighty God, we are most heartily sorry for having willfully and selfishly sinned against Thy Holy Name. We detest all our sins; mostly because these offend Thee . . . Who art all good and deserving of all our love. Amen.

2 Chronicles 7:14 "If my people which are called by My name, shall humble themselves, and pray, and seek My face, and turn from their wicked ways, then will I hear from heaven, and will forgive their sin, and will heal their land."—God—KJV

I gotta lot of *respect* for tradition, but a *passion* for truth! (Taken from the wise words of Robert Duvall in the movie *Seven Days* in Utopia;

INTRODUCTION

As a teenager, growing up on a small eastern Iowa farm, I was just like everyone else; even though I didn't know it at the time. I thought I was different; and, that no one felt like I did: it was scary. I wanted to be liked, have friends, be popular, and above all get to drive my dad's car. At the same time, I never wanted to do anything that would embarrass my parents. Yet, I must confess I did many things my parents never knew about: or, I thought they didn't. My philosophy was simple: *'don't get caught.'* Such words as; computer, Aids, I-Pod, I-Phones, Global Positioning Satellite, texting, email, digital, television, transistors, digital camers, cholesterol, stereo, e-mail, security cameras, disposable cameras, penicillin, the Interstate, were all unknown entities when I was a teenager, and this list grows daily!

In our home we did have the *luxury* of an old upright console wind up record player, which was a treasure! I had a few of those old thick records to play on this fine instrument. It was a top of the line console Victrola, made by Edison, with one of those heads you could turn from side to side to accommodate the luxury thick or thin records. It was such a pleasant surprise when I discovered the new electronic recordings of the big band era sounded so very natural, even though there were no electronics in the old wind up Victrola. I was afraid the new electronic recordings would sound like those old fashioned records, but they didn't! They sounded just great!

In my teen years, I would frequent the popular teenage hangout of the area, and we would take turns contributing nickels for the nickelodeon to play the great sounds of those big bands. Here we could dance until closing time. I listened to all the popular music of the day; or, to put it another way, I liked what everyone liked—most of the popular music of that day. This was really all the music to which we were exposed. No higher goals were considered, for we lived for the joys and thrills of the moment. Basically, this is what most young people do, unless there are strong moral and Christian values exemplified and taught by the parents.

My oldest brother George said to me, "Turn off that Glenn Miller Band, and listen to the classics: Beethoven, Mozart, Bach, etc." He also said "The Big Bands would never last: they are too noisy, neurotic and repetitious." Of course I strongly disagreed! I just could not understand what could possibly be wrong with the popular music of my youthful days. On the other hand, I was certainly aware that much of the music was not good, morally and/or audibly! However, this was very mild as compared to what passes for the sounds called music in today's world.

We had a cleaning girl (Betty) in our home from time to time, a classmate of mine, who helped my mother with house work when needed. Whenever she was in our home, I enjoyed giving her a hard time. I would tune in to the University of Iowa Classical music station KSUI, in Iowa City and turn up the volume as loud as possible; all this just to tease and irritate Betty as she went about her cleaning duties. I felt it was worth it, because she kept yelling to me "turn that noise down!" It made me laugh . . . it was fun, even though I also hated, what to me, were those weird screechy sounds coming from the classical music station. Actually, I was only proving how foolish and uncouth I was!

A few years later I dated Mildred Blezik, from Maquoketa. She was a lover of classical music . . . even opera. She had one of those new fangled stackable record chargers with a transmitter in her home. This made it possible for us to sit in my dad's car on her driveway, and listen to the music of Richard Wager. I put up with this music out of respect for Mildred, because I really liked her. In my mind, Mildred stood for the finer qualities of life. Without even realizing it at the time . . . I was being exposed to music I didn't understand or appreciate, but I was beginning to enjoy it. Even now, I tear up a bit when listening to Wagner's Tristan Und Esolde—the Liebestod (German for 'the Love Death' music). All this brings back many precious memories as I recall the emotions this triggered in Mildred, as I watched her get so emotionally involved in the music. Now, after all these years, I can honestly confess, that to me . . . Wager's music is some of the most dramatic, powerful, inspirational, beautiful, calming, emotional, and meaningful music ever written.

In college, many of my friends were lovers of the classics. A few enrolled in the music appreciation course that was offered. For some reason, I didn't enroll, even though this was supposed to be a snap course. I was really too busy with my pre-med science courses, with their required lab hours. Over the years, especially after the big bands disappeared, I turned toward the classical music: music that has indeed lasted the test of time. I did not like the 'individualistic' trend music was taking in the 50's. The big band groups were beginning to fade away, as other talented individuals and small groups, were taking over. This was more profitable. There weren't so many on the payroll.

Basically, I believe that anyone can grow to enjoy that to which he or she is exposed. This is all part of growing up. But know this . . . one's growth need not stop at any point along the way. We are always under construction! Reach for that which is lasting: reach for that which is higher. Don't get stuck with the status quo. I shall never forget what our dear friends, Roger and Beverly Swanson have above the door to their home: *"Home is where your story beings."* This is worth remembering for a lifetime! Do not let your story begin in the streets, at private parties, or in someone's car! And do not be afraid to make changes in your life by climbing up a rung or two on the ladder, from what turns your friends on. There is always room for improvement. There is always a goal for which to reach. You may never reach your goals, but remember there is always room for growth. Be an innovator, not an imitator! Those things to which we are exposed in this life, to a large degree, determine what we are becoming. We are persons under construction on this earth! Let us think of God as the architect, and

Jesus as the contractor through which—**Philippians 4:14** reads *"I can do all things through Christ which strengtheneth me."* KJV

Billy Graham's wife Ruth, told him what she wanted on her tombstone (not the pizza). She said: "As we drive down the highway, we often see the sign *"Road construction ahead."* Soon, Billy and Ruth would come to another sign—*"End of construction . . . thanks for your patience."* Ruth turned and said to Billy *"These are the words I want on my tombstone: End of construction, thanks for your patience."*

Persons may change their life style, but they are always going to be sinners, hopefully recognizing their need of accepting Jesus Christ as their Lord and Savior. The basic requirement for the individual is to know, or at least try to know, his or her personal needs. Making *better decisions* with an eye on your future, is then more likely to happen, rather than to just live for the moment. And also remember, your basic needs are to be met in <u>communion</u> with the Lord, friends and family! This is why we have Churches; but, we also have other groups asking for support; gangs, clubs, bars, lodges, etc. These groups are as diverse as they are endless. Persons of similar interests band together for support: this is human nature. The fact is we do need one another, whether we are out for good or bad!

BACKGROUND TO THE ART OF WORSHIP

The Church is made up of individuals who have found communion with Christ. The Church is the Body of Christ! The Church is really the hands of Christ to a lost world that is looking in all the wrong places to fulfill their personal needs! **Acts 4:12** *"Salvation is found in no one else, for there is no other name under heaven given to men by which we must be saved."* NIV

When a person becomes part of Christ's fellowship, we are more likely to be aware that we have good works to do in His Name.

Now look at **John** 14:**12** *"Verily, verily, I say unto you, He that believeth in me, the works that I do shall he do also; and greater works than these shall he do; because I go unto my Father."* KJV

And this is followed by our Lord's Great Commission: **Matthew 28:18** *"And Jesus came and spake unto them, saying, All power is given unto me in heaven and in earth. 19 Go ye therefore, and teach all nations, baptizing them in the name of the Father, and of the Son, and of the Holy Ghost: 20 Teaching them to observe all things whatsoever I have commanded you: and, lo, I am with you always, even unto the end of the world. Amen."* KJV

Before we can respond to the above Scripture, we first need to become the *body of Christ* **United**, regardless of the denomination with which we are affiliated. Until we do this, the world looks at the Church as being divided into segments, and is therefore irrelevant to their needs! Persons outside the church need to see in us something they need and want for their own lives. As for now however, we *appear* to be in the state of confusion. We often act like a dysfunctional family.

This material has not been written to be critical or dogmatic about the various worship styles. **This has been written to reflect what I consider to be <u>Biblical Worship</u>.** You may disagree, and this is your prerogative.

Please understand what is written herein has grown out of my experiences as a pastor. I don't mean to sound dogmatic, so please forgive me if I do. You may disagree, and even get angry, and this is your privilege, because we all try to defend our positions. Quite often I refer to the same Scriptures, and even similar examples as I jump from one subject to another. However, never let us say "**<u>let us agree to disagree</u>**," for this means our minds are closed! Thank you for reading on, and may the peace of God be with us all!

Before we go any further, we need to understand the background of what happened at the very beginning of **Mankind's history**.

WHAT DID GOD SEE WHEN HE LOOKED UPON THE EARTH IN THE BEGINNING?

God looked at His creation and called it good. In **Genesis 1:31** *"God saw every thing that He made, and, behold, <u>it was very good</u>. And the evening and the morning were the sixth day."* KJV

However, not long after Creation, *The Fall of Man* took place. Then God took another look at the earth, and <u>things were no longer good</u>.

THE FALL OF MAN

Genesis 1:17 *"God created man in his own image, in the image of God he created him; male and female he created them."* NIV

Genesis 2:8,9 *"Now the LORD God had planted a garden in the east, in Eden; and there he put the man he had formed. 9 And the LORD God made all kinds of trees grow out of the ground—trees*

that were pleasing to the eye and good for food. In the middle of the garden were (the tree of life) and the tree of (the knowledge of good and evil)."

Genesis 2:15-17 *"The LORD God took the man and put him in the Garden of Eden to work it and take care of it.* **16** *And the LORD God commanded the man, "You are free to eat from any tree in the garden;* **17** *but you must not eat from the tree of the knowledge of good and evil, for when you eat of it you will surely die."* NIV

Genesis 3:1-5 *"Now the serpent was more crafty than any of the wild animals the LORD God had made. He said to the woman, "Did God really say, 'You must not eat from any tree in the garden'?"* **2** *The woman said to the serpent, "We may eat fruit from the trees in the garden,* **3** *but God did say, 'You must not eat fruit from the tree that is in the middle of the garden, and you must not touch it, or you will die.'* **4** *"You will not surely die," the serpent said to the woman.* **5** *"For God knows that when you eat of it your eyes will be opened, and you will be like God, knowing good and evil."* NIV

Question: Is the *tree of life* and the *tree of knowledge of good and evil* one and the same tree? Answer: These are not the same tree, because *Man did eat of the tree of knowledge of good and evil*, and was therefore **barred** from the Garden of Evil, *lest he eat of the tree of life and live forever in his sinful state.*

Genesis 3:24 *"After God drove the man out, he placed on the east side of the Garden of Eden cherubim and a flaming sword flashing back and forth to guard the way to the tree of life".* NIV

TREE OF LIFE

We shall **not** always be forbidden to eat of the tree of life as we see in the following passages.

Proverbs 15:4 *"The tongue that brings healing is <u>a tree of life,</u> but a deceitful tongue crushes the spirit. "* (Words of wisdom) NIV

Proverbs 3:18 *"<u>She (wisdom) is a tree of life</u> to those who embrace her; those who lay hold of her will be blessed."* NIV

Revelation 2:7 *"He who has an ear, let him hear what the Spirit says to the churches. To him who overcomes, I will give <u>the right to eat from the tree of life,</u> which is in the paradise of God."* NIV (Note: Then we shall live forever in a sinless state)

OH OH, WE ARE IN TROUBLE!

The Fall of Man is an event that took place near the beginning of Man's history. Mankind was bent on disobeying the Lord God. This is called sin. So now we turn to the basic problem in our lives, and look at this situation honestly and realistically! Unless we first realize we are sinners in need of help, and confess this fact that we are sinners with <u>needs</u>: we are walking in endless circles, and not going anywhere! **Romans 3:23** *"For all have sinned, and come short of the glory of God."*

Instead of humbling ourselves, we are determined to keep living in our world of false security. We are trying to survive like a fish out of water. We are looking in all the wrong places for the correct answers! We are smothered by the same corrupt philosophy of life that William Ernest Henley wrote about in "**Invictus.**"

"Out of the night that covers me, Black as the Pit from pole to pole, I thank whatever gods may be for my unconquerable soul. In the fell clutch of circumstance I have not winched nor cried aloud. Under the bludgeonings of change my head is bloody, but unbowed. Beyond this place of wrath and tears looms but the horror of the shade, and yet the menace of the years finds, and shall find, me unafraid. It matters not how strait the gate, how charge with punishments the scroll. I am the

master of my fate: I am the captain of my soul." We really need to put a question mark at the end of that sentence!

We are far from being the captain of our own souls: we are sinners in need of God's grace! All we have to do is watch the news, give an eye to what is around you, or just look at the history of Man; and, be sure to include Biblical times. Better yet, look at yourself in the mirror (not a glass one, but see your reflection through Holy Scripture). We've got problems!

Let us look at more of Man's background, and the problems this has caused. When we fail to recognize we have *needs*, we do not go looking for answers . . . because we are of the mistaken opinion that I'm Ok and your OK: but we aren't!

We know that persons do not basically change without the Holy Spirit's help, for we all have sinned, and continue to sin, and miss the mark in seeing the glory of God in our daily lives. If we do change our way of life, we are still sinners in need of God's plan of salvation offered through Christ. We need God's help, along with the help of others (in fellowship and communion within Christ's Body the Church): yet, the fact of sin in our lives remains . . . we are still sinners! That part of us has not changed. As a professor told us in seminary, "We are forgiven and forgiving sinners!"

It is of vital importance to see what happened at the foot of Mt. Sinai where Moses (up in the Mt.) had received the tablets with the 10 engraved Commandments (not suggestions)!

WHAT HAPPENED AT THE FOOT OF MT. SINAI?

satan is the father of lies. Let us take a good hard look at what went on at the foot of Mt Sinai, while Moses was up in that mountain, where God gave His Ten Commandments (not suggestions) to Moses. The people thought Moses had forsaken them since he stayed on Mt. Sinai for such a long time (40 days).

Exodus 32:1-35 *"When the people saw that Moses was so long in coming down from the mountain, they gathered around Aaron and said, 'Come, make us gods who will go before us. As for this fellow Moses who brought us up out of Egypt, we don't know what has happened to him.' 2 Aaron answered them, 'Take off the gold earrings that your wives, your sons and your daughters are wearing, and bring them to me.' 3 So all the people took off their earrings and brought them to Aaron. 4 He took what they handed him and made it into an idol cast in the shape of a calf, fashioning it with a tool. Then they said, 'These are your gods, O Israel, who brought you up out of Egypt.' 5 When Aaron saw this, he built an altar in front of the calf and announced, 'Tomorrow there will be a festival to the LORD.' 6 So the next day the people rose early and sacrificed burnt offerings and presented fellowship offerings. Afterward they sat down to eat and drink and got up to indulge in revelry. 7 Then the LORD said to Moses, 'Go down, because your people, whom you brought up out of Egypt, have become corrupt. 8 They have been quick to turn away from what I commanded them and have made themselves an idol cast in the shape of a calf. They have bowed down to it and sacrificed to it and have said, 'These are your gods, O Israel, who brought you up out of Egypt.' 9 'I have seen these people,' the LORD said to Moses, 'and they are a stiff-necked people. 10 Now leave me alone so that my anger may burn against them and that I may destroy them. Then I will make you into a great nation.' 11 But Moses sought the favor of the LORD his God. 'O LORD,' he said, 'why should your anger burn against your people, whom you brought out of Egypt with great power and a mighty hand? 12 Why should the Egyptians say, It was with evil intent that he brought them out, to kill them in the mountains and to wipe them off the face of the earth'? Turn from your fierce anger; relent and do not bring disaster on your people. 13 Remember your servants Abraham, Isaac and Israel, to whom you swore by your own* *self: I will make your descendants as numerous as the stars in the sky and I will give your descendants all this land I promised them, and it will be their inheritance forever.'* **14** *Then the LORD relented and did not bring on his people the disaster he had threatened.* **15** *Moses turned and went down the mountain with the two tablets of the Testimony in his hands. They were inscribed on both sides, front and back.* **16** *The tablets were the work of God; the writing was the writing of God, engraved on the tablets.* **17** *When Joshua heard the noise of the people shouting, he said to Moses, 'There is the sound of war in the camp.'* **18** *Moses replied: 'It is not the sound of victory, it is not the sound of defeat; it is the sound of singing that I hear.'* **19** *When Moses approached the camp and saw the calf and the dancing, his anger burned and he threw the tablets out of his hands, breaking them to pieces at the foot of the mountain.* **20** *And he took the calf they had made and burned it in the fire; then he ground it to powder, scattered it on the water and made the Israelites drink it.* **21** *He said to Aaron, 'What did these people do to you, that you led them into such great sin?'* **22** *'Do not be angry, my lord,' Aaron answered. 'You know how prone these people are to evil.* In the following verses from Exodus, **notice** how **satan** through the people, convinces even Aaron, the brother of Moses, to do his bidding. **23** *They said to me, Make us gods who will go before us. As for this fellow Moses who brought us up out of Egypt, we don't know what has happened to him.'* **24** *So I told them, 'Whoever has any gold jewelry, take it off. Then they gave me the gold, and I threw it into the fire, and out came this calf!'* **25** *Moses saw that the people were running wild and that Aaron had let them get out of control and so become a laughingstock to their enemies.* **26** *So he stood at the entrance to the camp and said, 'Whoever is for the LORD, come to me.' And all the Levites rallied to him.* **27** *Then he said to them, 'This is what the LORD, the God of Israel, says: Each man strap a sword to his side. Go back and forth through the camp from one end to the other, each killing his brother and friend and neighbor.'* **28** *The Levites did as Moses* *commanded, and that day about three thousand of the people died. 29 Then Moses said, 'You have been set apart to the LORD today, for you were against your own sons and brothers, and he has blessed you this day.' 30 The next day Moses said to the people, 'You have committed a great sin. But now I will go up to the LORD; perhaps I can make atonement for your sin.' 31 So Moses went back to the LORD and said, 'Oh, what a great sin these people have committed! They have made themselves gods of gold. 32 But now, please forgive their sin—but if not, then blot me out of the book you have written.' 33 The LORD replied to Moses, 'Whoever has sinned against me I will blot out of my book. 34 Now go, lead the people to the place I spoke of, and my angel will go before you. However, when the time comes for me to punish, I will punish them for their sin.' 35 And the LORD struck the people with a plague because of what they did with the calf Aaron had made."* NIV

It is interesting to see how Cecil B. DeMille, (whom many believe to be the greatest director, producer, and writer in Hollywood at that time), interpreted what has just been read from the book of Genesis above, in terms anyone can understand. **What happened at the foot of Mt. Sinai the day God gave the Ten Commandments to Moses**.

Cecil B. DeMille's movie "Ten Commandments", vividly describes what happened at the foot of Mt. Sinai as follows:

"Go . . . get thee down Moses, for thy people have corrupted themselves. And the people rose up to play, and did eat and drink. The wicked were like a troubled sea, whose waters cast up mire and dirt. They sank from evil to evil, and were viler than the earth. They were as the children of fools and cast off their clothes. There was rioting and drunkenness. They have become servants of sin. And there was manifest all manner of ungodliness and works of the flesh even adultery and lasciviousness, uncleanness, idolatry and rioting . . . vanity and wrath, and they were filled with iniquity and vile affections. And Aaron knew that he had brought them to shame."

Some may argue that Cecil B. DeMille has overstated the facts. Regardless of what you, and others may think, please know that **we still have The Golden Calf in our midst today!**

Running ahead of God, as we also are prone to do, the people turned away from Jehovah God, to do just as they pleased. God was very angry with His people, and if it weren't for the intercession of Moses, God would have destroyed them all at that time. Joshua made a bold statement, but many did not follow his personal decision to serve the Lord. **Joshua 24:15** *"And if it seem evil unto you to serve the LORD, choose you this day whom ye will serve; whether the gods which your fathers served that were on the other side of the flood, or the gods of the Amorites, in whose land ye dwell: but as for me and my house, we will serve the LORD"*

Thankfully, God only destroyed those who would not follow Him in faith and obedience. God has every right to destroy His people when they refuse to follow Him! First, God destroyed His people in the great flood which covered the earth in the days of Noah and the Ark. God has promised to never destroy His people by a flood again . . . thus the rainbow. It is important to keep in mind that God has another promise of destruction for rebellious Man: next time it is not by water, but by fire! **II Peter 3:3** *"First of all, you must understand that in the last days scoffers will come, scoffing and following their own evil desires."* **4** *And saying, Where is the promise of his coming? for since the fathers fell asleep, all things continue as they were from the beginning of the creation. 5 But they deliberately forget that long ago by God's word the heavens existed and the earth was formed out of water and by water. 6 By these waters also the world of that time was deluged and destroyed. 10 But the day of the Lord will come like a thief. The heavens will disappear with a roar; the elements will be destroyed by fire, and the earth and everything in it will be laid bare. "11 Since everything will* *be destroyed in this way, what kind of people ought you to be? You ought to live holy and godly lives* 12 *as you look forward to the day of God and speed its coming. That day will bring about the destruction of the heavens by fire, and the elements will melt in the heat.* 13 *But in keeping with his promise we are looking forward to a new heaven and a new earth, the home of righteousness.* 14 *So then, dear friends, since you are looking forward to this, make every effort to be found spotless, blameless and at peace with him."* NIV

THE ART OF WORSHIP
PRAYERFULLY CONSIDER THIS

Before reading further, please prayerfully consider the words found in **Hebrews 12:28-29** *"Therefore, since we are receiving a kingdom that cannot be shaken, let us be thankful, and so <u>worship God acceptably</u> with reverence and awe, 29 for our "<u>God is a consuming fire.</u>"* NIV

Man is bent on doing as he pleases:—**Romans 1:25** *"Man has changed the truth of God into a lie, and worshipped and served the creature more than the Creator, who is blessed for ever. Amen."* KJV

We all need to ask ourselves two vitally import questions: *"<u>Is the way I worship acceptable to God in light of Scripture?</u>"* Also . . ."<u>Do I really know God as revealed in Scripture?</u>"

We are all in the same boat . . . no one can judge us but God! However, know this: **worship is mentioned 191 times in the Bible**, so <u>how we worship must be important</u>! No one can ever come to the point of knowing all about God! We so flippantly say "O Yes, I know God and believe in Him." God reveals Himself through Scripture, and through the presence of His Holy Spirit, and of course through Jesus who came to live amongst us as God in the flesh.

John 1:14 "The Word became flesh and made his dwelling among us. We have seen his glory, the glory of the one and only Son, who came from the Father, full of grace and truth."

Also, we can see God's handiwork through His creation.

Psalm 19:1-4). *"The heavens declare the glory of God; and the firmament sheweth his handywork. 2 Day unto day uttereth speech,*

15

and night unto night sheweth knowledge. 3 There is no speech nor language, where their voice is not heard. 4 Their line is gone out through all the earth, and their words to the end of the world." KVJ

The most effective way to know God is through Jesus. But who among us can truthfully say we really know Jesus, and do His will perfectly as we walk in His steps, following His teachings. As concerning God the Father in heaven, the Apostle Philip shows his lack of understanding.

In **John 14:9** *Jesus saith unto him* (Philip), *Have I been so long time with you, and yet hast thou not known me, Philip? he that hath seen me hath seen the Father; and how sayest thou then, Show us the Father?* KJV

Remember: Jesus was God in the flesh reconciling the world to Himself. However, God the Father, was still in heaven controlling His world.

In **2 Corinthians 5:19** we read *"To wit, that God was in Christ, reconciling the world unto himself, not imputing their trespasses unto them; and hath committed unto us the word of reconciliation."* KJV

Philippians 2:7-9 *"But made himself of no reputation, and took upon him the form of a servant, and was made in the likeness of men: 8 And being found in fashion as a man, he humbled himself, and became obedient unto death, even the death of the cross. 9 Wherefore God also hath highly exalted him, and given him a name which is above every name."* KJV

Colossians 1:15 *"The Son is the image of the invisible God, the firstborn over all creation. 16 For in him all things were created: things in heaven and on earth, visible and invisible, whether thrones or powers or rulers or authorities; all things have been created through him and for him. 17 He is before all things, and in him all things hold together."* KJV

God is also the Creator who said: **Genesis 1:26** *"Then God said, 'Let us make mankind in our image, in our likeness, so that they may rule over the fish in the sea and the birds in the sky, over the livestock* *and all the wild animals, and over all the creatures that move along the ground.'"* NIV

Notice the use of words such *us* and *our* in this Scripture. (Herein is the Trinity.) He knows all . . . and has put everything we could possibly think about into its proper order! He is simply pure HOLYNESS . . . so know this: be satisfied with that, and treat God with due respect! Give unto God your very best! The hymn *"Give of Your Best to the Master"* has it right!

The often used term *awesome* is an adjective describing how we feel about God, but it doesn't even come close to defining God. This is a term we mistakenly use, for lack of a term that better describes how we feel about God. We can never add to God or detract from God. He is the Great **I AM**—Jehovah; Yahweh, Elohim, Shaddai, Adonai, Jehovah-Jireh, and the list goes on. These are a references to the name by which God identified Himself when Moses stood before Him on Mt. Sinai. God said *"I Am That I Am"*; i.e., God told Moses that He had no beginning and no end, *"I just Am!"* How do we respond to the One unfathomable God, who loves us! Think about this! **Psalm 46:10 *"Be still, and know that I am God; I will be exalted among the nations, I will be exalted in the earth."***

If we really knew all about God, our brains would explode, or as I often put it "We would blow a fuse." However, we can know as much as any human can comprehend, about God's Son without getting into the problem of blowing the fuse of our brain!

When it comes to worshiping God, we better keep a humble spirit. If you are of the opinion that churches need to have two or more services to worship God in different ways; one to attract the younger generation, another to attract older people, as we attempt to be people pleasers: know this . . . you cannot please everyone. God did not send more than one Jesus to earth to tell us how to worship: one to lead persons to worship one way, and another to lead people in to worship in another way. We simply need to humble ourselves and seek the Lord while He may be found. Isaiah **55:6** *"Seek ye the LORD while he may be found, call ye upon him while he is near:"*

There is only one God for all people! The emphasis should not be about pleasing people: rather about our being acceptable and pleasing to God. We should not come into the Lord's House to give vent to our peculiar likes and dislikes when worshiping the Lord. We come to corporate worship to calm our world laden, uneasy and troubled spirits, as we give attention to the Word of God and sing music that highlights God's glory and grace. There are 6 basic segments to the corporate worship service. **(1)** The spoken word, **The Sermon**); **(2) The Offering** to support the Lord's Mission work at home and around the world (See stewardship, page 62) **(3) Prayer; (4) Holy Communion** (when offered), to remember Christ's death and suffering as the Lamb of God Who taketh away the sin of the world. When we celebrate Holy Communion it is done to help worshipers *remember* what God through Christ has done for us to make it possible for our sins to be, not only forgiven: but forgotten. **Isaiah 43:25** *"I, even I, am he who blots out your transgressions, for my own sake, and remembers your sins no more."*

John 1:29 *"The next day John seeth Jesus coming unto him, and saith, Behold the Lamb of God, which taketh away the sin of the world."*

In **11 Corinthians 1:25** Jesus said: *"this do ye, as oft as ye drink it, in remembrance of me."*

Luke 22:19 *"And he took bread, and gave thanks, and brake it, and gave unto them, saying, This is my body which is given for you: this do in remembrance of me."*

I Corinthians 11:24 *"And when he had given thanks, he brake it, and said, Take, eat: this is my body, which is broken for you: this do in remembrance of me."*

I Corinthians 11:35 *"After the same manner also he took the cup, when he had supped, saying, This cup is the new testament in my blood: this do ye, as oft as ye drink it, in remembrance of me.";*

(5) Scripture; and, **(6) Singing**. These 6 are the basic segments of corporate worship.

There are other special services in the church beside corporate worship. We know them as Marriage, through which to propagate believers within the family, and the Funeral for the purpose of giving comfort to the grieving family from the Word of God. Funerals give a sense of closure to the grieving family and friends as well. We go to funerals for three specific reasons: **(1)** We know the deceased individual. **(2)** We want to express our sympathy and support to family members. **(3)** We hope to hear, a message from Word of God, from where our comfort and hope comes!

There is also a personal benefit as well when attending a funeral service. Everyone needs to understand that his or her turn is coming up sooner than he or she may realize, and there is hope for them as well from the Word of God. Everyone needs to hear the salvation plan of God for His children! This cannot be overstressed, and it is not up for debate! Funeral messages are important!

Also: *We need to shed ourselves of the idea that at a funeral we celebrating the life of John Doe.* We seem to think we are giving comfort to family members of the deceased by using the word *celebrate*. Do those attending a funeral really feel like celebrating? We may feel we are celebrating when we discuss all the attributes and idiosyncrasies of the diseased, which may even bring a chuckle from some. This may give mourners a temporary comfort. But, the loss of a loved one is never a time to celebrate. And who an honestly say the word *celebrate* refers to the deceased *new destination* (His or Her new life)? Who is able to judge the deceased's destination? However we do know the deceased Christian is in the hands of the Lord. **John 11:26** *"Whosoever liveth and believeth in me shall never die."* God does not lie! Death is really a sleep until the day of judgment. Remember Jesus said that Lazarus was sleeping, **John 11:11** *"These things said he: and after that he saith unto them, Our friend Lazarus sleepeth; but I go, that I may awake him out of sleep."*

But for those outside of Christ: God is the only Judge! Our modern culture is trying unrealistically, to ease the fact of death with words that sound pleasant, however there is no comfort in a false sense of security! Only truth from the Word of God can bring peaceful comfort. Psalm 121:2 *"My help (comfort) cometh from the Lord, who made heaven and earth."* Let us give that comfort to the bereaved.

Whenever we gather for corporate worship, weddings, or funerals, it must be based upon the Word of God, and not upon personalities and/ or social status. Please know it is not God who needs defending: it is we who need defending against the whiles of the devil. **Ephesians 6:11** ***"Put on the whole amour of God that ye may be able to stand against the wiles of the devil."*** Our defense is in the Word of God!

What is written herein is not a collection of how I personally feel worship should be conducted, although you will no doubt think this is the case. Scripture is the norm and foundation for worship: not me! My opinions do not matter! The Church belongs to God: not us! (**Church**=universal Church: **church**=the local congregation). At all times, we are answerable to God. The Church should be guided by God, but this can only come to fruition by studying and knowing the Word of God in Scripture under the guidance of the Holy Spirit. The Church is not a man made organization, to be guided by the endless whims of its membership. The Church is a **living organism** . . . the Body of Christ, subject to God in everything. The purpose of the Church is found in **Matthew 28:18-20** in the Great Commission ***"And Jesus came and spake unto them, saying, All power is given unto me in heaven and in earth. 19 Go ye therefore, and teach all nations, baptizing them in the name of the Father, and of the Son, and of the Holy Ghost: 20 Teaching them to observe all things whatsoever I have commanded you: and, lo, I am with you always, even unto the end of the world. Amen."***

WORSHIP AS AN ART

Art is:

1. *the production of something beautiful or extraordinary—the Christian man or woman. (The Believer!)*
2. *seen in paintings, drawings, sculptures, etc.*
3. seen in one's skills; and abilities:

WHAT IS WORSHIP?

The **American Heritage Dictionary** defines worship as: ***The reverent love and devotion accorded a deity, an idol, or a sacred object.*** Worship involves the ceremonies, prayers, or other religious forms by which love toward God, and our fellow humans is expressed. An empathy is created to allow others at worship to be attracted to Christ the Savior. Worship is the act of giving praise to the Lord. It is to serve the Lord. It is to give glory to His Name. Worship also is a medium through which people may be drawn closer to Jesus Christ their Savior! At worship we feel true love and adoration for God, and are thankful to God for His the plan of salvation offered through His Son Jesus the Christ.

One can always consult **Webster's Dictionary** for the precise meaning of worship (adore, idolize, esteem worthy, reverence, homage, etc.). Yet to truly define worship proves more difficult, because it is **both an attitude and an act.**

I believe it is vital to our generation to consider a few suitable definitions of the word **worship**. I believe this is urgently important because too often we throw words around (even theological ones) without stopping to define exactly what we are trying to say, and this is confusing.

A.W. Pink in his Exposition of the Gospel of John defined worship as, *"A redeemed heart occupied with God, expressing itself in adoration and thanksgiving . . . Worship, then, is the occupation of the heart with a known God, and everything which attracts the flesh and its senses, detracts from real worship."*

Worship, is the response of redeemed Man (Mankind and Womankind), who has been created in God's image. This does not mean that we look like God! It does mean however, that God's attributes have also been given to us. We have **will, intellect, and emotion**, even as God Himself has these attributes. Since the Fall of Man, these attributes have been badly damaged in each of us. We are fallen creatures! In our worship we gratefully respond to God, our Lord and King, who has created us in His image. His redemptive work through Jesus Christ must bring a quite humble attitude and response to individuals who seek to worship God!

Worship is about God's children, who respond to a recognized Creator, in a way whereby EVERY single part of our being accepts, with grateful hearts, the redemption that was accomplished by Jesus Christ on the Cross of Calvary. Worship is directed to the Lamb of God, Who is worthy of all praise! May He be glorified in ALL things and worshiped properly. Therefore: nothing in our worship should be considered **programmatic**, so as to result in applause. Applause this directs our attention away from the Father, and turns our praise toward one another, and the one or ones, who has just praised God in song or instrumental music. As inspirational as it may be, and should be . . . we are totally responsible to God's Holy Spirit working in us, otherwise we are at an entertainment hall. Don't settle for how the world does it! The response of the majority is not always right! You don't have to clap your hands just because someone next to you does!

"The Sunday Morning Corporate Worship service is often tailored to suit the endless peculiar tastes of those present. We need to be keenly aware that we do not surrender the Lordship of Jesus into the hands of un-churched seekers." (The Truth War, by John McArthur, page 152)

PRACTICING THE ART OF WORSHIP

The surgeon practices his art whenever he or she steps into the operating room. The surgeon dare not just *wing it*. He must follow specific rules! The musician is practicing his or her art when learning the instrument of choice, but it takes years for this to bear fruit. It takes long hours of practice, discipline, and a true love for the instrument that a person may be seeking to master. Becoming an attorney, a teacher, a pastor, a mechanic, or whatever your goal may be as you seek to lead a productive life—takes time, discipline, and determination. Your goals and dreams must not be compromised or sidetracked. You are becoming an artist, or to say it another way, *a professional* in your chosen field of service.

Nothing is more important than becoming an artist in the area of worshiping the Lord God: we are His creation! We belong to God, and so does everything we think we own: it all belongs to God. Without God we would have nothing. One of the pastors at the Crystal Cathedral has recently reminded us: our home belongs to God, our car belongs to God, and even the air we breathe belongs to God. God as Creator has given us all we need for this life. What we do with this life is up to us, and others who inspire us. The worship of God commands and deserves the very best we have to offer: through the words we speak, and the talents God has given us. Cultivate your worship habits. Learn to give unto God the best you have. Remember the hymn: ***Give of Your Best to the Master.***

Give of your best to the Master
Give of the strength of your youth
Throw your soul's fresh, glowing ardor
Into the battle for truth
Jesus has set the example
Dauntless was He, young and brave

Give Him your loyal devotion
Give Him the best that you have

Give of your best to the Master
Give of the strength of your youth
Clad in salvation's full armor
Join in the battle for truth

Give of your best to the Master
Give Him first place in your heart
Give Him first place in your service
Consecrate every part
Give, and to you shall be given
God His beloved Son gave
Gratefully seeking to serve Him
Give Him the best that you have

Give of your best to the Master
Naught else is worthy His love
He gave Himself for your ransom
Gave up His glory above
Laid down His life without murmur
You from sin's ruin to save
Give Him your heart's adoration
Give Him the best that you have

Romans 12:1-8 *"Therefore, I urge you, brothers, in view of God's mercy, to offer your bodies as living sacrifices, holy and pleasing to God—this is your spiritual act of worship. 2 Do not conform any longer to the pattern of this world, but be transformed by the renewing of your mind. Then you will be able to test and approve what God's will is—his good, pleasing and perfect will. 3 For by the grace given me I say to every one of you: Do not think of yourself more highly* *than you ought, but rather think of yourself with sober judgment, in accordance with the measure of faith God has given you. 4 Just as each of us has one body with many members, and these members do not all have the same function, 5 so in Christ we who are many form one body, and each member belongs to all the others. 6 We have different gifts, according to the grace given us. If a man's gift is prophesying, let him use it in proportion to his faith. 7 If it is serving, let him serve; if it is teaching, let him teach; 8 if it is encouraging, let him encourage; if it is contributing to the needs of others, let him give generously; if it is leadership, let him govern diligently; if it is showing mercy, let him do it cheerfully."*

Only you can decide what *your best* may be! Hopefully, your best 'likes' are not summed up in the music of Led Zeppelin, Michael Jackson, Prince, the Beatles, Elvis, or any of the endless upcoming misused and misguided talents, that have cropped up in the past, and are endlessly showing up in the future. These sounds and antics are out of place for the worship of God: they are out place everywhere!!! Nevertheless these sounds are for programs or performances: not for the worship of God! We need to be on guard at all times, against turning Godly worship into human glorification through our choice of music. Even the big band sounds were and are not suited for the worship of God! The vast majority of what passes for music in this century is certainly not fit for worship, no matter what religious words we may affix to them. How can we get back to uplifting, inspirational music? (See the Definition of Music, page **126ff**).

I refer to worship as an art, since art always necessitates many disciplines. An artist must use his or her time wisely, and exercise a regimen that develops or improves one's skill: having the ability to bring out one's best with what God has given. When speaking of Worship as an Art, do not make the mistake of thinking one can approach God and gain His favor through rituals, practice and disciplines, although these are vitally important for our sake. Special gimmicks and presentations during corporate worship do not equal a service that is acceptable to

God. The pastor, worship committee, or some individual may feel they have come up with something new and exciting, even different, that is special and memorable for the congregation at worship. These gimmicks or presentations do not mean we have pleased God in our worship, nor does all this mean we are winning young or adult souls for Christ. These may attract crowds, but is our goal to get individuals to repent and confess personal sin; or, are we more interested in a nice program for the people? We are not saved by works or rituals, although rituals are a fine guideline! The Art part comes into play when we are able to acknowledge our need to worship as God directs—in such a manner that is acceptable and pleasing to Him. Corporate worship should **inspire individuals**, even though it may be programmatic material. This is most acceptable! Anything that inspires and promotes soul searching; resulting in repentance is what we are about! Our mission is not to be devising new and different programs that we think are cleaver, and even exciting so as to get the youth and/or the congregation involved. The **faithful** dramatization of Scripture is very inspiring and helpful in corporate worship. However, we have so rationalized ourselves into thinking we <u>always</u> need to come up with something new for public appeal. Churches should void doing as Commercial advertisers are always doing: that is to constantly come up with something new (labels and packaging, etc.) to entice people to purchase their old familiar product. Remember, most of what advertisers are telling us, to put it plainly, is misleading. The Church is not in the world to mislead the populace to suit our own purposes! Our goal, while we are in the world; is to witness to the Word, even though the world may hate us. **John 15:19** reads: *"If ye were of the world, the world would love his own: but because ye are not of the world, but I have chosen you out of the world, therefore the world hateth you."*

BIBLICAL WORSHIP

First: **Biblical worship** comes only from a heart that has been redeemed. The word worship basically means that one show a deep respect to God, and then to prostrate (humble) one's self before God Who is Holy. *Biblical worship* is true worship and is highlighted in **John 4:23** *"But the hour cometh, and now is, when the <u>true worshippers</u> shall worship the Father in spirit and in truth: for the Father seeketh such to worship him."*

Worship is made up of 6 basic parts; Prayer, Preaching, The Lord's Supper, the Offering, Scripture and Singing. These are all Biblical, and our worship must be based upon the Word of God. We don't have the prerogative to decide for ourselves how we are to worship. We always need to remember that true or Biblical Worship is not oriented toward entertainment, therefore; applause is unnecessary. Applauding, once the worship service has started, is an interruption to the flow of worship and inspiration. God is the One to Whom we are to direct our uninterrupted thoughts, attention and praise! Be alive and awake . . . we are honoring and worship the Lord, who has given us a way out of our sin . . . THIS IS EXCITING!!!!! Show this in one's worship!

Second: **Biblical worship** is that which comes from a heart that desires **only God**. *Third*: **Biblical worship** desires to know as much about God as a person can know of God in this sinful, mortal flesh.

NON-BIBICAL WORSHIP

<u>Non-Biblical worship</u> is the result of a heart that is—*First of all:* non-redeemed. *Secondly*: Non-Biblical worship comes from the mind of one who does not confessedly desire God as directed in Scripture, but who needs *"<u>additions</u>"* of one sort or another, to make this worshiper <u>feel good, and be</u> <u>the center of attention</u>. And *Thirdly:* this kind of worshiper does not want to know much about God, for this could

take away their control of how worship should express itself. This non-Biblical worship is an expression of all that **appeals to the flesh** and detracts from true worship and inspiration, making it impossible for God to speak to the individual, because this person is so involved with self. This person thinks he or she already knows more about God than others do! This includes (1) **Ignorant Worship**, (2) **Vain Worship** and (3) **Will Worship**.

An example of (1) ***Ignorant Worship*** is found in Paul's experience when he was in Athens as recorded in **Acts 17:21-25 and 30** *"For all the Athenians and strangers which were there spent their time in nothing else, but either to tell, or to hear some new thing. 22 Then Paul stood in the midst of Mars' hill, and said, Ye men of Athens, I perceive that in all things ye are too superstitious. 23 For as I passed by, and beheld your devotions, I found an altar with this inscription, TO THE UNKNOWN GOD. Whom therefore ye ignorantly worship, him declare I unto you. 24 God that made the world and all things therein, seeing that he is Lord of heaven and earth, dwelleth not in temples made with hands; 25 Neither is worshipped with men's hands, as though he needed any thing, seeing he giveth to all life, and breath, and all things; 30 And the times of this ignorance God winked at; but now commandeth all men every where to repent."*

(2) **Vain Worship** is exemplified in **Matthew 15:9** *"But in vain they do worship me, teaching for doctrines the commandments of men."* We do not have the right to put into our worship our own wishes, mannerisms, personalities, likes and desires!

(3) **Will Worship** is exemplified for us when we look at Cain's offering to the Lord: he gave to the Lord what he wanted and what suited him. **Genesis 4:3-7** *"And in process of time it came to pass, that Cain brought of the fruit of the ground an offering unto the LORD. 4 And Abel, he also brought of the firstlings of his flock and of the fat thereof. And the LORD had respect unto Abel and to his offering: 5 But unto Cain and to his offering he had not respect. And Cain was very wroth, and his countenance fell. 6 And the LORD said unto*

Cain, Why art thou wroth? and why is thy countenance fallen? 7 If thou doest well, shalt thou not be accepted? and if thou doest not well, sin lieth at the door. And unto thee shall be his desire, and thou shalt rule over him." satan wants to rule your life and make it difficult for you to properly worship the Lord. In the temptation of Jesus we read these words: **Matthew 4:8** *"Again, the devil took Jesus to a very high mountain and showed him all the kingdoms of the world and their splendor. 9 All this I will give you, he said, if you will bow down and worship me. 10 Jesus said to him, Away from me, Satan! For it is written: 'Worship the Lord your God, and serve him only.'"*

In the first place satan did NOT have the power to give Jesus the kingdoms of the world, even if Jesus had worshiped him. If satan couldn't get Jesus to worship him, and he couldn't, then his (satan's) next opportunity was to try and dupe us into worshiping him, but how do we do that? Our temptation is to get us to bow down and worship either satan or ourselves—this is satan's plan. However, he doesn't care who we worship so long as it isn't God or His son Jesus! satan will pull every stop to get our attention so as to receive our worship. Note: we may not call it worship, but this is he best term I know of to use at this point. We are too sophisticated to ever admit that we would or could ever worship satan!

Therefore be careful in the way you worship and praise the Lord. It is a very dangerous experience to feel self righteous over the way one worships. We may have a content and good feeling about ourselves in the way we worship (I am so happy and content with myself in the way I worship, and so are my friends). Remember pride cometh before a fall. **Proverbs 16:18** *"Pride goeth before destruction, and an haughty spirit before a fall."* **KJV**

We must remember that for everything that is good, the evil one (satan) will have an alternative that is bad, false, evil, and stands in contradiction to the Holiness of God. The devil and his followers are accomplishing this very well in our lives, in our homes, and in our churches throughout Western Christianity, and around the world as well. The results have become more and more painfully visible, and this is making Christianity a source of ridicule in much of the world. It also opens the door for other religions of the world: particularly the Islam religion, that is growing more rapidly in the United States than is Christianity.

Understanding the meaning of worship in our world today is vitally necessary, because too many just think they are worshiping God, Whom they really do not know. They have heard what others have said about God, but really do not know Him from experience. Therefore, they also have a false understanding of Biblical Worship. All who read this should examine their heart in the light of God's Word, to see if their worship is Biblical or Non-Biblical! Biblical Worship becomes a reality when one approaches God with a humble heart and spirit . . . ready to quietly hear what God is saying through each segment of the worship experience.

Worship goes back to an old Anglo-Saxon word, which had in its root form the idea of ascribing **worth** to someone or something. One dictionary defines it as 'courtesy or reverence that is paid to worth.' Who is more worthy than God!

People are incurably religious. They are going to worship something or someone (an idol or god). Everybody in the world worships. The rich, the poor, the religious, and the heathen all give reverence, courtesy, and ascribe worth to someone or something in the world today. Every religion is based on worship. Every life is based on worship. Every desire is based on the worship of something or someone.

William Temple, who was a former Archbishop of Canterbury in England, said, "Worship is to quicken the conscience by the holiness of God; to feed the mind with the truth of God; to purge the imagination by the beauty of God; to open the heart to the love of God; to devote the will to the purpose of God."

William Temple is really saying something we all need to think about carefully:

(1) The only way to God, is though <u>Biblical Worship</u>, that can quicken or making alive a dead conscience. This can only be done when we are brought face to face with **the holiness of God**. However, many consciences have been seared with a hot iron (**I Timothy 4:2**). Mere drivel and fluffy messages will never bring a person to face the reality of a Holy God!

(2) The only way to find our <u>conscience awakened,</u> is by feeding the mind with the **Truth of God's Word**. Nice stories, and quips telling you that you can be a better person, is not what Scripture teaches! Dwight L. Moody said, "It is not our comments about God's that is powerful . . . it is the Word of God itself from the Holy Bible that has power."

(3) The only way to feed the mind is through a <u>purging of the imagination,</u> which is only accomplished by feasting our entire minds and hearts on the beauty of God. This requires that we stop thinking of ourselves more highly than we ought to think, and silently concentrate on an <u>uninterrupted</u> worship service. **Psalm 46:10** *"Be still and know that I am God!"* Let go of yourself and let God dwell in your total being. Worshipers must stop thinking about what they have seen on television, or how some individuals dress or look in the church, or what they are having for dinner. Purge the mind! Concentrate!

(4) The only way to have our imaginations purged from the filth of the world is by having our <u>hearts opened by the love of God</u>. We can only understand and appreciate the love of God, when we realize what it is, and from which we have been saved (our sin and rebellion). This should quiet worshipers down in humble repose, and not allow for shallow and repetitious ditties performed by sincere, well meaning worship leaders. In the use of all music that is sung, remember to concentrate on the words . . . are they Biblically (theologically) correct?

(5) The only way that we can give evidence of a heart that is filled with love for God: is to <u>surrender our will to God</u>. In a nutshell, this means that we must be willing to die to self daily, to crucify the flesh with all its temptations and desires, and submit to our Heavenly Master.

We cannot worship God rightly, by trying to make everyone do things the way we want them done! This creates division, chaos, hard feelings and a divided congregation. However, please note the words found in **Matthew 10:34** where Jesus is saying *"Do not suppose that I have come to bring peace to the earth. I did not come to bring peace, but a sword."*

We don't want to hear these words: yet how true it is. The truth of God has brought about an endless chain of divisions . . . hurt feelings . . . and it is still happening. Look at **Luke 12:53** *"They will be divided, father against son, and son against father, mother against daughter, and daughter against mother, and mother-in-law against daughter-in-law and daughter-in-law against mother-in-law."* Have we not seen this throughout the history of mankind?

CORPORATE WORSHIP

Please remember what has been written so far. *Worship is really practicing the presence of God.* It is first of all, an every day experience: not just for one hour on Sunday. *Corporate worship* is what takes place when we gather on the Lord's Day, with others in the church of our choice. It is difficult to worship God, if we insist on adding to the worship experience, whatever we feel would be inviting, different, and new to ourselves and to others. We must **stand** for something, or we will **fall** for anything. God deserves the best we have. After all, God gives us life moment by moment. But the human problem is that we give to God our leftovers. John Wesley wrote about tradition! **"Without tradition we would be lost to the maze of our man made rules."**

Worship is giving praise to God, not only in the corporate worship setting, but in our daily lives as well. Most all of the hymns in the hymnal give solid praise to the Lord. Think of the great hymn *'The Church's One Foundation.'* There is only one foundation upon which the Church is built and that is Jesus Christ, the Son of God, and our Savior. Much of this generation's newer contemporary compositions give praise to the Lord God as well. The contemporary songs *'Higher Ground'* or *'People Need the Lord!'* are great examples. Admittedly, these are more solo oriented than for congregational singing. Inspirational music such as this brings one to a peaceful quietness and joy! Applause should seldom, if ever, be a part of the corporate worship experience, and this cannot be overemphasized!

The sound of clapping hands breaks the spirit of inspiration, which leads to motivation! Actually, complete silence after a 'mountain top experience' is the greatest compliment one can give to a soloist, who has just brought the congregation to a high plane of worship and inspiration! If you really hear this music, and are inspired because the person is doing his or her best with God given ability, you will desire to be still, silent, and deep in thoughts of inspiration and praise to God. Music sooths and quiets the heart, and lifts us up in gratitude to the Lord. Music is the universal language! Music embraces all generations and cultures.

Is the Lord pleased when we enter His house of worship? In our worship we follow the rituals, whether they be contemporary or traditional, and we are all guilty of taking, much too casually, the fact that our presence in the house of the Lord is to worship our Savior. **Psalm 96:9** reminds us to *"Worship the LORD in the splendor of his holiness; tremble before him, all the earth."* NIV It is doubtful that we have done much trembling in this our day!

Someone may come before the Lord in torn jeans (which is fine if this is all one has), but hopefully, everyone attending worship will have a high enough regard and respect for the Lord, so they will desire to dress accordingly. When we dress with the best we have, and stand before the Lord, we feel better, look better, and maybe even sound better when we sing! But never look down on the person who cannot afford the same quality of clothing as you may have. Worship is not a style show!

At worship, the sounds of the world cannot quicken the spirit and bring peace and joy to the heart. Also, please remember . . . **Cliché's quickly loose meaning and effectiveness. They end up as meaningless, thoughtless, and boring phrases.** What can be done about this? Why not just be yourself? Don't put on a mask and pretend you are something other than yourself.

There is an old movie depicting people going to worship, that I have shown in some of my churches. I think the title of this movie is *"The Mask."* It is no longer available. In the movie, as people enter the church, each would take a mask from the conveniently located box at the entrance to the church. Everyone carefully put on his or her mask to wear throughout the corporate worship service. When the worship was over, and it is time to leave the church, the mask was placed back into the box from which it was taken when leaving the sanctuary. Nothing of consequence happened in this particular church, until one day, one daring soul took off his mask during the worship experience. This caught on, and soon everyone at worship had taken off his or her mask, and were just being themselves. Now they became a congregation, ready to be inspired through God's Word, and inspirational music. Sometimes it is really difficult to take off our masks to just be ourselves, without feeling intimidated or judged by others.

In our sanctuaries, we are *in the House of the Lord!* In our daily lives we are living *in the presence of the Lord!* We can't really get away from God, even if we wanted to rid ourselves of Him.

Psalm 139:7 *"Whither shall I go from thy spirit? or whither shall I flee from thy presence? 8 If I ascend up into heaven, thou art there: if I make my bed in hell, behold, thou art there. 9 If I take the wings of the morning, and dwell in the uttermost parts of the sea; 10 Even there shall thy hand lead me, and thy right hand shall hold me."*

Hebrews 10:31 *"It is a fearful thing to fall into the hands of the living God."* KJV Like it or not . . . this is exactly where we are . . . in the hands of the living God.

Psalm 91:1-7 *"The LORD reigns, let the earth be glad; let the distant shores rejoice. 2 Clouds and thick darkness surround him; righteousness and justice are the foundation of his throne. 3 Fire goes before him and consumes his foes on every side. 4 His lightning lights up the world; the earth sees and trembles. 5 The mountains melt like wax before the LORD, before the Lord of all the earth. 6 The heavens proclaim his righteousness, and all the peoples see his glory. 7 All who worship images are put to shame, those who boast in idols—worship him, <u>all you gods</u>!"* NIV

What does the phrase "<u>all you **gods**</u> mean?" The serpent (devil) was right . . . we have become little gods, knowing good and evil! **Genesis 3:5** *"For God doth know that in the day ye eat thereof, then your eyes shall be opened, and ye shall be <u>as gods</u>, knowing good and evil."* KJV

We have partaken of the forbidden fruit (rebellion against God to do as we please). Humans have worshiped and are worshiping most anything and everything. Our passions are what we place first in our lives. Whatever we place first in our lives, we worship, so what is your passion? Be careful. There is but One God. We gods are to worship the only God. If this is unclear to you, please remember what the serpent (satan) said to Eve *"You shall be <u>as gods</u> knowing good and evil."* Yes, <u>we are all little gods</u> in need of the one Lord God Jehovah! So take off the mask and worship honestly. Admit your need: The forgiveness and salvation of the Lord.

It has been said that Christianity is the transformation of rebels into worshipers of God. If this be the case, then it is imperative for the Christian to know and understand what constitutes Biblical worship. Halley, in his Bible Handbook, asks "Why do we go to church?" Then he records a very profound statement: "Worship is **not about us**: it is **all about God**." Give this some serious thought before moving on! We come into the House of the Lord, hopefully with humble and profound gratitude for all God has given, and is giving us! Worship is the recognition that God has given us this life along with <u>eternal life in</u>

35

<u>Christ</u>. This merits our veneration of God (worship) in all we do each day as well, not just on Sundays, or special days we set aside. Worship is *primarily* not for us: we have a knack for stepping in the way as a road block to God's intervention. *Worship is for God, and directed toward God, and is all about God*; <u>then we reap the benefits of being a child of God</u>. God calls us through His Holy Spirit. When we worship, we are responding to God; His love for all He has done, and is doing for us.

When it comes to music in the worship service, I am fully aware that most persons, who listen to rap, rock and roll, and heavy medal sounds, etc., will dogmatically say "This is the music that I love. It makes me jump around (dance), and feel good, I clap my hands, and I get my feet a tappin. It is also what all my friends are listening to as well. I wish I could play the guitar, keyboard, or drums, so I could perform and be like those musicians I see in the movies and on television: then perhaps I could even play for worship at my church." **There is a time and place for performing, but the corporate worship in the sanctuary of the Lord is not one of them.**

Remember: in worshiping God, as Halley reminds us, it is not about you when you worship, **it is all about God: all that God has done for each one of us.** Count your blessings one by one, and you will soon discover the list is endless and you are totally incapable of remembering them all! When a person looses sight of this truth, that worship is all about God: then there is the danger to focus too much on *stylistic preferences*. It is not a matter of what the individual likes, or what makes people feel good, or even alive and free from boredom: it is all about God! At worship we, through the format of the service, want to be acceptable unto God. He is the focal point of the corporate worship experience! Once a person comes to know God from His Word in Scripture, the light suddenly dawns: God is not boring . . . and you are not bored any more. You know why you have come to the corporate worship experience. If you is bored at worship, please take a good honest look into your heart. You are not at worship to be entertained.

Worship is not a program. You are at worship for one reason: to praise the Lord for His unwarranted Grace, love and forgiveness. And while at worship an individual will learn more about the God of grace and mercy. One must always remember the words of Isaiah, **chapter 6 and verse 1** *"In the year that king Uzziah died I saw also the Lord sitting upon a throne, high and lifted up, and the train of his robe filled the temple."*

In worship **it is the Lord who is exulted, and not the worshiper.** **The worshiper is inspired!** We do not attend worship to be prideful, but to see the Lord God high and lifted up. A person receives joy at worship when one brings before the Lord a heart that is humble, grateful, and open to the leading of the Holy Spirit! See the Lord as High and Holy. Don't come to worship with your eye on the clock, or what you want to eat for dinner, etc.

HOW DID JESUS WORSHIP?

This is a good question, but there is nothing in the Bible that tells us how Jesus worshiped. Did Jesus worship himself, or pray to himself? After all He was God in the flesh. **II Corinthians 5:19**, where we read: *"God was in Christ reconciling the world unto himself, not imputing their trespasses unto them, and hath committed unto us the word of reconciliation."*

Scripture does make it very clear that Jesus did pray to the Father in heaven, and He did this very often as He went about His Father's business. There was, and is, a definite oneness between the Father and Jesus! We shall never know in detail what Jesus did while worshiping His Heavenly Father. We do know He was the Word (God) made flesh. **John 1:1** *"In the beginning was the Word, and the Word was with God, and the Word was God."* and **John 1:14** *"The Word became flesh and made his dwelling among us. We have seen his glory, the glory of the one and only Son, who came from the Father, full of grace and truth."*

The entire life of Jesus was an act of worship and prayer. One could say, "This is how Jesus worshiped." He was always practicing the presence of the Father. We do know how Jesus prayed in simple understandable language. Of course we have the example of *'The Lord's Prayer,'* which He taught to His disciples. In the Garden of Gethsemane, Jesus left most of his disciples behind and went some distance from them to pray. He took take Peter, James and John with Him a bit further, but even then, Jesus separated from these 3 and went on a bit further to pray to His Father. To Jesus, prayer was strictly between the Father and Himself. He prayed to His Father, seeking the strength to be able to fulfill His mission. Jesus prayed to the Father, asking that this cup (His fast approaching crucifixion) be removed from him. **Matthew 26:39** reads *"And He (Jesus) went a little further, and fell on His face, and prayed, saying, O My Father, if it be possible, let this cup pass from me, <u>nevertheless not as I will, but as thou wilt.</u>"*

Jesus was always being about His Father's Business, wherever He was! When He taught (or some may say preached), Jesus was direct in what He said. He spoke as one who had authority (and He did have this authority, as the Son of God).

Jesus relied heavily upon the use of parables to get his message across to those who had ears to hear. He could have been the proudest person on earth, but He did not behave in this manner!

We also know that Jesus taught in the synagogue: **Luke 4:14-19** *"Jesus returned to Galilee in the power of the Spirit, and news about him spread through the whole countryside. 15 He was teaching in their synagogues, and everyone praised him. 16 He then went to Nazareth, where he had been brought up, and on the Sabbath day he went into the synagogue, <u>as was his custom.</u> He stood up to read, 17 and the scroll of the prophet Isaiah was handed to him. Unrolling it, he found the place where it is written: 18 <u>The Spirit of the Lord is on me, because he has anointed me to proclaim good news</u> to the poor. He has sent me to proclaim freedom for the prisoners and recovery of sight for the blind, to set the oppressed free, 19 to proclaim the year of the Lord's favor."*

As concerning worship, Jesus did say in **John 4:23** *"But the hour cometh, and now is, when the true worshippers shall worship the Father in spirit and in truth: for the Father seetheh such to worship him."* KJV Jesus also knew, as He served His Heavenly Father, that He was sent amongst us with a mission. Philippians 2:**6** *"Who, being in very nature God, did not consider equality with God something to be used to his own advantage; 7 rather, he made himself nothing by taking the very nature of a servant, being made in human likeness. 8 And being found in appearance as a human being, he humbled himself by becoming obedient to death—9 Therefore God exalted him to the highest place and gave him the name that is above every name, 10 that at the name of Jesus every knee should bow, in heaven and on earth and under the earth, 11 and every tongue acknowledge that Jesus Christ is Lord, to the glory of God the Father."* NIV

As we consider how Jesus might have worshiped, it may be helpful to think about what Jesus did not do in the synagogue. When He went into the synagogue, He showed only the highest regard and respect toward His Heavenly Father. Even as a 12 year old boy, Jesus debated with the Church leaders of his day. **Luke 2:42** *"And when he was twelve years old, they went up to Jerusalem after the custom of the feast."* **Matthew 7:29** *"And He taught as one who had authority."*

Never is there any indication that Jesus busied Himself by *chatting* away in the synagogue, dancing or waving His arms, telling jokes, and shouting for joy, or talking about the weather. Jesus took life seriously. He never wavered because He knew His faithfulness was for our benefit! Jesus was teaching, praying, and being faithful, i.e., being about His Father's business. Jesus did, however, take what we would call **drastic actions** to set the people straight. This was serious business, not a casual club. Jesus knew the *inner self and obedience is of more importance than outward demonstration.* **1 Samuel 15:22** *"And Samuel said, Hath the LORD as great delight in burnt offerings and sacrifices, as in obeying the voice of the LORD? Behold, to obey is better than sacrifice, and to hearken than the fat of rams."* KJV

A Bible professor in college told us that Jesus could be as hard as nails against what was happening in the temple area and world of His day. Jesus raised his voice in <u>righteous</u> indignation. Listen as he drove out the money changes from the temple area: **Matthew 21:12-13** *"Jesus entered the temple area and drove out all who were buying and selling there. He overturned the tables of the money changers and the benches of those selling doves. 13 'It is written,' he said to them, 'My house will be called a house of prayer, but you are making it a den of robbers.'"* NIV

Jesus said: "My house (sanctuary) is a <u>place</u> (house) <u>of prayer</u>." Jesus was demonstrating the fact that the religious leaders of His time, needed to get their ducks in a row so to speak.

Matthew 12:33-37 *"Make a tree good and its fruit will be good, or make a tree bad and its fruit will be bad, for a tree is recognized by its fruit. 34 <u>You brood of vipers, how can you who are evil say anything good?</u> For out of the overflow of the heart the mouth speaks. 35 The good man brings good things out of the good stored up in him, and the evil man brings evil things out of the evil stored up in him. 36 But I tell you that men will have to give account on the day of judgment for every careless word they have spoken. 37 For by your words you will be acquitted, and by your words you will be condemned."* NIV

However, we can be certain Jesus did conduct Himself with total respect, dignity, and faithfulness toward His Heavenly Father: and never went about changing His <u>*methods,*</u> as we are endlessly doing in our churches today, to please individuals.

ISAIAH'S CALL
GIVES US THE PATTERN FOR WORSHIP

There is only one very **crucial passage** in Scripture that outlines what worship is, and how the worshiper should react when at worship. This is found in **Isaiah 6:-1-9**. *"In the year that King Uzziah died, I* *saw the Lord seated on a throne, high and exalted, and the train of his robe filled the temple.* **2** *Above him were seraphs, each with six wings: With two wings they covered their faces, with two they covered their feet, and with two they were flying.* **3** *And they were calling to one another: "Holy, holy, holy is the LORD Almighty; the whole earth is full of His glory."* **4** *At the sound of their voices the doorposts and thresholds shook and the temple was filled with smoke.* **5** *"Woe to me!" I cried. "I am ruined! For I am a man of unclean lips, and I live among a people of unclean lips, and my eyes have seen the King, the LORD Almighty."* (Confession) **6** *Then one of the seraphs flew to me with a live coal in his hand, which he had taken with tongs from the altar.* **7** *With it he touched my mouth and said, "See, this has touched your lips;* (cleansed your filthy mouth) *your guilt is taken away and your sin atoned for."* **8** *Then I heard the voice of the Lord saying, "Whom shall I send? And who will go for us* (Father, Son and Holy Spirit)*?" And I said, "Here am I. Send me!"* **9** *He said, "Go and tell this people:"* NIV

Do your see a pattern here?

Looking carefully at these verses we find **(1)** <u>**The sight of God**</u>, **(2)** <u>**The need for repentance**</u> (Woe is me, Isaiah cried out before the Lord). Isaiah admits that he is a man of unclean lips, and he lives among people of unclean lips, but now his eyes have seen the Lord Almighty. Isaiah knew he had sin in his life, but now, before the presence of God, it could not be set aside any longer, so he confesses his sin before God. Then Isaiah is cleansed by one of the seraphs who flew to him with a live coal, and his hands and his lips were made clean, **(3)** <u>**Forgiveness**</u> . . . *his guilt is taken away and his sin forgiven.* For Christians, it is the blood of Jesus that cleanses us from all sin. Following Isaiah's having seen the Lord, and confessing his sin, along with the need for repentance: next Isaiah experiences a call from the Lord for service. **(4)** <u>**A call to service!**</u> Isaiah is prepared and willing to serve the Lord. "Here I am, send me!"

In, our own experience of worship, we should recognize the **PRESENCE OF GOD**, and this leads to **REPENTANCE**, and **CONFESSION**, and next comes God's **INTERVENTION** (**God's FORGIVENESS AND GRACE**), and this is followed by **SERVICE** to the Lord. Our guilt is taken away! Are we willing to do anything about such grace of the Lord in our own lives?

We often sing *'Here I Am, Lord.'* But do we realize that in this hymn, God is calling us . . . and hopefully, we are responding to His call. He wants to send us, as He did Isaiah. Look carefully at these words. Do we mean what we are singing? This why we need to sometimes read the words without the music to see what we are really saying! This would be to our benefit!

Verse:

I, the Lord of sea and sky, I have heard my people cry. All who
dwell in dark and sin, My hand will save.
I, who made the stars of night, I will make their darkness bright.
Who will bear my light to them? Whom shall I send?
I, the Lord of snow and rain, I have borne my people's pain. I have
wept for love of them. They turn away.
I will break their hearts of stone, Give them hearts for love alone. I
will speak my words to them. Whom shall I send?
I, the Lord of wind and flame, I will send the poor and lame. I will
set a feast for them. My hand will save.
Finest bread I will provide, 'Til their hearts be satisfied. I will give
my life to them. Whom shall I send?

Chorus:

Here I am, Lord. Is it I, Lord? I have heard you calling in the night.
I will go, Lord, if you lead me. I will hold your people in my heart.

So we really mean what we are singing?

It is a great practice to repeat things over and over again in different words, because this helps us remember! So . . . I repeat: At corporate worship: **(1)** We see God in His Holy Temple (Church). We respect the holiness and sanctity of where we are and our behavior should give witness to this awareness. **(2)** We are aware of the fact that we are sinners, but forgiven sinners, no matter how long we have been Christian. **(3)** We find forgiveness and grace in Christ. Forgive us our sin as we forgive those who sin against us. **(4)** Finding **inspiration** we are **motivated** to go out into the day world, and witness. **If this does not happen, our worship needs to be revised!**

In the Lord's house, we are gathered to see God seated upon His throne, in His temple (church) which was filled with His glory. If, at worship, we are seeing everything other than the Lord in His Holy Temple, then our worship is all an act (hypocritical), boring and judgmental! Jesus has promised that where two or three are gathered in His Name, He is present (**Matthew 18:20**). Of course we see others, and the way the sanctuary looks etc, and this is the reason the worshiper needs to concentrate on the primary reason for worshiping—to see the Lord in His Holy Temple. Admittedly this takes concentration, determination and humbleness of heart. Remember, the Holiness of God was accompanied by heavenly beings around Him, as His servants. Also present, was a great choir singing "Holy, Holy, Holy." The singing of the heavenly choir was so **profoundly beautiful, glorious**, and **unworldly**, that **the very Temple shook to its foundations.** Here Isaiah was in the very presence of God the Father. Isaiah felt so unworthy (so should we) at being in the presence of God. He could not help but confess—"Woe is me, for I am a sinner."

It is difficult to see and feel the presence of God when so much is going on all around us! God tells us to be still (quiet down, be attentive, and receptive) and know that He is God. That is the key! The real justification for our being in the House of the Lord is to receive God's forgiveness, and to be fitted for the service of the Lord. We gather together for inspiration; it is a learning experience; and for the much needed fellowship with others!

Isaiah heard the call and responded, but was told something he did not understand, or want to hear. God said to **Isaiah 6:10** *"Make the heart of this people fat, and make their ears heavy, and shut their eyes; lest they see with their eyes, and hear with their ears, and understand with their heart, and convert, and be healed."* KJV

A cross reference at this point may be helpful. **Matthew 13:15** reads: *"For this people's heart has become calloused; they hardly hear with their ears, and they have closed their eyes. Otherwise they might see with their eyes, hear with their ears, understand with their hearts and turn, and I would heal them."* NIV

After a meaningful worship experience, we know that all people will not always respond to our witness. But this should not hinder our faithfulness to the Lord!

The Israelites, would not listen to God's Word, until their cities were destroyed, and their country is an utter wasteland, and the people were taken to Babylon as slaves. Yet a remnant did survive. Although Israel is invaded again and again and destroyed, yet Israel was as a tree cut down, whose stump still lives to grow again. I might add, so will the Church of Christ, if we are willing to fulfill God's call in our lives.

The tree in the back yard of the parsonage in Prairie City, Iowa, where we were living, had died. Some men of the church came and cut the tree down to ground level, after all it had no life in it any more: so we thought. Year after year, this stump kept growing new branches that looked like an unsightly bush. I thought we could take care of that bushy growth that came back each year from the dead tree, by trimming it back to the ground and then heavily covering it with a load of soil. This mound of soil would be an ideal spot for growing flowers. The soil was to prevent further branches from growing back; but, it didn't work! It took at least 3 years before the dead tree finally stopped sending forth new shoots. Finally, the tree remnant stopped growing.

So far as God's people are concerned, there shall always be that remnant of the faithful, but they are not, and never shall be unsightly growth! And nothing the world can do, will ever kill or stop the remnant of the Lord from proclaiming the truth of God, nor stop the saints from serving the Lord!

WORSHIP AT THE DUKE UNIVERSITY CHAPEL

An article appeared in The **United Methodist Reporter for April of 2011,** that was written by Andrew Thompson. I have included it here, in part, for your thought and consideration. He calls it as he sees it. He writes: "Go into one of those services (at Duke University Chapel), and you'll see liturgy done the way God intended. The hymns, the prayers, even the way the Scripture is read all made you feel a little like you're standing on the edge of heaven. It is worship designed to glorify the Creator of the universe."

In the same issue of the United Methodist Reporter, April 15, 2011, is another enlightening and thought provoking article, written by columnist Donald Haynes. He asks: "Do we understand that <u>Christianity is Christ</u>?" He continues saying "**<u>The supreme purpose for living</u> is to find and to know God**, and no religion provides the portrait of God that is comparable to Jesus."

THE WORSHIP SERVICE

When it comes to worshiping the God of revelation, it must **not** be done with pride and demonstration, so as to call attention to oneself as being more Christian than those who sit quietly, i.e., a worshipers actions should not be offensive or a distraction to other worshipers. Humility and reverence is hard to come by! The Scripture says **we may approach God freely and with confidence.** This is not a pride thing! Thank the Lord for this confidence! However, when one approaches the Lord it is not the same as approaching your neighbor or friend with confidence. God is Lord and when we come before Him in prayer or at worship it must be done with reverence! The Lord is Holy! This reminds me of that great sacred composition written by Cesar Frank *"O Lord most Holy."* Yes . . . *the Lord is most Holy*!

Ephesians 3:12 *"In Him (Jesus) and through faith in Him we may approach God with freedom and confidence."* NIV

However remember what Paul the Apostle said on one of his missionary trips. **1 Corinthians 2:33** *"And I was with you in weakness, and in fear, and in much trembling."* KJV

Here Paul is speaking about his ministry. He could come before the Lord with freedom and confidence because of his relationship with Jesus. Paul was seeking to present the gospel to those around him, but he did it in *weakness, in fear, and trembling.* He was humble before people, and strong in the Lord.

This generation needs to know what it is to come before the Lord in fear and trembling. Fear is a healthy emotion. Remember: the great hymn *"Amazing Grace"* begins the second stanza with these words: "Twas grace that taught my heart to **fear**, and grace my **fears** relieved."

1 John 4:18 *"There is no fear in love; but <u>perfect love casteth out fear</u>: because fear hath torment. He that feareth is not made perfect in love."* KJV

Yes . . . *perfect love casts out fear*, but who amongst us has *perfect love*? So, there is a place for genuine fear if we are out of line . . . however, our hope is in Christ's perfect love for each of us. We can indeed approach God freely and with confidence, knowing that He hears us!

In Philippians 2:12,13 *"Wherefore, my beloved, as ye have always obeyed, not as in my presence only, but now much more in my absence, <u>work out your own salvation with fear and trembling</u>. 13 For it is God which worketh in you both to will and to do of his good pleasure."*

THE BEST FORMAT FOR WORSHIP IS THAT WHICH ALLOWS FOR *INSPIRATION*: FOLLOWED BY *MOTIVATION*, AND *THIS LEADS TO ACTION*! Then, and only then, we have the right to *feel good.* Let the people at concerts, performances and sporting events shout and wave their hands. Church is where we surrender self to the Spirit of the Living God. **Psalm 46:10** *"Be still, and know that I am God;"* and if this cannot be done in our worship, where else can it be better demonstrated.

Let it be clearly understood before going any further: worshipful entertainment may be inspirational, and can also lead to motivation (motivation is needed to get things done). But we need to take great care in planning for worship, that it does not become *just entertainment.* Some movies are entertaining, as well as inspirational; however we are not worshiping when at the movies. I have heard many people say, as they were leaving the theater, "That was such a good movie. I enjoyed it so much," . . . as they wipe the tears from their eyes. So now the word emotional enters the scene. We need controlled emotion at worship. Weep because of your sin. Weep for joy because of inspiration received. We need to make room for tears of repentance. Weeping cleanses the soul! Weeping is a personal and private event, so do it quietly so as not to disturb others.

Because inspiration is of prime importance, once the worship experience is begun, **nothing should break or shatter the flow of inspiration!** This means that announcements and greetings should be taken care of <u>before</u> worship begins. The **Prelude** . . . signals the beginning of the worship experience. Worship from then on is made up of various tried and tested formats such as: The Introit, Prayers, The Singing Hymns, The Responsive Scripture Readings as a congregation, Confession, The Scriptures, Special Music, Responses found in Rituals, The Tithes and Offerings, The sermon, and Holy Communion.

There should be no happenings that break the spirit of inspiration (announcements and the shaking of hands is over). In fact, the shaking of hands (Passing the Peace) at corporate worship, should also be eliminated all together. There is plenty of time to shake hands before and after worship. Let's not make worship seem like a free-for-all. I personally have never liked "The Passing of God's Peace" as part of the worship service. If it must be done . . . do not do it during the flu season! Most worshipers don't say "May the peace of God be with you" to one another while shaking hands anyway. What they do say is "Good morning, or how are you today, etc. This segment of worship looks and sounds like a free for all.

If we stretch **Psalms 98** and **100** (see page 143ff) to justify shouting in church, or the waving of hands, during worship, not only is our personal worship shallow and erotically demonstrative, but a disruption to other worshipers who find inspiration in the stillness of God's whispers. Too much of our worship is given over to persons who have structured the worship service to fit personal psychological ambitions and needs. We are in corporate worship to praise God, not human talents and personalities! Yet, we are so very thankful for human talents and abilities!

An admission must be acknowledged at this point. It is so easy to sing the words of a hymn when at worship, and at the same time think about one's plans for after worship, etc. How many times have you recited *The Lord's Prayer*, while thinking of how hungry you are, and where you are going to eat after church, etc? Our minds do have a strong tendency to wonder: as do our eyes.

Worship takes concentration, commitment, dedication, and humility! This is where the art of dethroning-self comes into play.

Let these next Bible passages speak, then examine your heart . . . .

Matthew 15:9 *"They worship me in vain; their teachings are but rules taught by men."* NIV

And now this prayer: "God keep me from imposing my personal preferences, and idiosyncrasies upon others who are seeking to worship the Lord."

Luke 4:8 Worship also has to do with **serving** the Lord: Jesus answered, **"It is written: *'Worship the Lord your God and serve Him only.'"*** NIV

God is to be worshiped in spirit and truth. We know God is Spirit, but what is truth? Truth is not something we can determine for ourselves and then proclaim to others, saying, "God has spoken to me, so now hear this great gem of truth God has given to me." This is done much too often. Even murders have been committed under the excuse that God has told someone to do it!

We had a member of our church in California who claimed that God told him to quit his well paying job (He was a civilian military photographer for the Navy) and go home and write a book. The book never materialized, and the last time I saw him, he was selling clothing in a department store. Be patient, and you will know when the Lord is directing your path, and not some personal desire or ambition: or even satan! It is so easy to say "This is the Lord's will," when it is really your own will!

It is a prideful thing to tell people that God has told you to do this or that. It gives one the feeling that he or she is very special and favored in the sight of God. God does speak to us, but in His still small voice. **God is truth**! Jesus is Truth Personified. There is but one truth for all humans! Yet, we are masters at telling half truths, or even worse: some outright lies. We are not the judges of *what is truth:* God is! Remain humble, receptive, and quiet, and God will speak to your soul. But pride does come before a fall. This is the reason we need to test all spirits and not run ahead of God!

True worship must to bring glory to God's name. **Revelation 15:4** *"Who will not fear You, O Lord, and* __*bring glory to Your name?*__ *For You alone are holy. All nations will come and worship before You, for Your righteous acts have been revealed."* NIV

Everyone must **worship God alone, even when at corporate worship in the church**. Each person, every couple, or family member who enters into worship, must realize each individual must worship for himself or herself. You cannot worship for someone else. So . . . no holding of hands or hugging or nestling in the worship experience. However, if your family member needs support to stand, put your arm around your love one, for this in itself depicts that the wholesome love of Christ is in the heart. We are in corporate worship to **WORSHIP**

GOD, as though we were alone, yet with loved ones. It is vitally important that we worship with our loved ones!

Applauding is out of line (except for rare situations, such as to encourage children: as they need this in their tender age), but soon they should realize applause **is not** their best compliment. The best compliment one can pay the individual, choir or group, is silence when have they have finished, for this lets the individual or group know they have touched and inspired the hearts of the congregation. They soon learn they are *up there* to praise God.

The Lord does not need our applause, all He wants from us is faithfulness and obedience! It is unlikely that applauding would be interpreted by most worshipers as praise to God after, someone has honored the Lord with some form of sacred music. Applauding after special music suggests that we have been entertained, and that we approve of the performance, and are thanking someone for doing a fine job. If we applaud just once for someone, it becomes almost impossible from keeping it from becoming the norm. Nothing is wrong with being entertained . . . this must be stressed! But remember, we are not in church and at worship to gain the approval and praise of Men. Worship is not about you: it is all about God! In only one sense is worship about you: you have made it to the church for worship. You are, from that point on, open to the Holy Spirit to interpret your prayers and needs, and to the voice of God as He speaks to your spirit. Inspiration takes place when all God's children are on the same page. We are all in need of God's forgiveness even though we are *forgiven and forgiving sinners* by the amazing grace of God: until the day we leave this earth. Then we are forever in God's hands and in His presence.

I realize some will disagree with what is written herein, but hopefully it will spur a few too think about applauding at worship. We are not called to be *yes* people, but we are called to be faithful, obedient, humble and truthful persons. Hear this again. What does the Lord require of us? **Micah 6:8 *"He hath shewed thee, O man, what is*** *good; and what doth the LORD require of thee, but to do justly, and to love mercy, and to walk humbly with thy God?"* KJV

If a segment of our worship happens to be entertaining, does this make that worship experience void? Not at all . . . IF IT IS INSPIRATIONAL! Inspiration comes in many forms. What may be of inspiration to one person may not be so to another. When a <u>guest soloist</u> inspires you because of his of her fine voice, or in the playing of an instrument etc., and the selection used was uplifting, should we applaud? Probably not, because the guest individual will have already come to he conclusion that the congregation does not applaud for anyone in a corporate worship service. If the congregation does applaud, make sure it does not become common practice! The best policy is: never applaud at worship, unless something very extraordinary has taken place. You will know when this happens. Always remember . . . once applauding for everyone who performs, gets started, it is next to impossible to stop. Applauding breaks the inspirational flow of worship in most cases! Don't start something you cannot stop! (See Applauding at Worship, page **203**)

In some congregations participants in the service are thanked after their part in the service is completed. This practice also becomes another interruption to a flowing service of praise to the Lord. If the pastor takes time to thank everyone for taking a part in the worship service, then he or she should remember to thank the congregation for being present? This would be ridiculous!

Holy Communion is the most sacred part of the worship experience. A few years ago I was privileged to attend a non-denomination experiment, held in Cincinnati, Ohio, to demonstrate how to update the celebration of Holy Communion, and our corporate worship services in general. On the large stage were sawhorses and several of those construction zone cones, accompanied by many flashing yellow road sign caution lights. The background for all that was on the stage was a large thin curtain with a bright light shining against it from the back, making it possible see the form of a female body dancing. Loud music was playing, and when all quieted down, the Scripture was read . . . well, it wasn't really Scripture. There were no Bibles around. Instead, the leader read sections from the daily newspaper. The idea being that congregation needed to know what is happening in the world before taking holy communion. The audience was patient with all these shenanigans, yet bewildered and curious. We wanted to stay to see what was coming up next, and when we would finally get to the Holy Communion part. It was around 45 minutes before, it was time for Holy Communion. The worship leader started sailing paper plates throughout the congregation. In turn, we were to sail a paper plate (if we could catch one) at others in the auditorium. This was supposed to be Holy Communion, but it was anything but holy. There were nurses at each entrance/exit to assist those who became ill, or who could not tolerate the noise in the auditorium. There were many who just had to get out of their seats and leave. Of course I did not get up to leave because I was too curious as to what would happen next. It was mass confusion!

Christians and churches need true unity; and, thinking of this unity it is helpful to compare ourselves, to a great symphony orchestra. We are supposed to be making beautiful music for the entire world to see, hear, understand, and appreciate. I fear, to the world we sound as though we are still tuning up for the music to begin. We sound confused! Everyone in the orchestra is trying to find where they are in the score, and if by chance we do, we are not quite on pitch. We need to remember that Jesus is the *Great Conductor*, and we need to be in tune with Him! We must get our lives in tune with others in the Lord's orchestra, so when it is time to make beautiful music we are ready. If our music is in harmony with the Word of God, and pleasing to God, then are we in harmony with one another as we worship! If each of us were to play our own tunes, ignoring others around us, pandemonium, confusion and chaos would result. This describes too many churches in our day. Soundboards, flashing lights, blasting sounds may be *cool*, however distractions such as these only adds to our problem. If Christians cannot get along with one another, this is not only tragic, it is disgusting!

There are no human answers in this complex world. Only God has the answer! And the Lord God says plainly: in **II Chronicles 7:14** *"If my people which are called by my name, shall humble themselves, and pray, and seek my face, and turn from their wicked ways; then I will hear from heaven, and will forgive their sin, and will heal their land." This is the Word of the Lord.*

We must get back to the Bible. Remember, "Amateurs built the Ark. Professionals built the Titanic." Christ built HIS Church: it doesn't belong to us!

Thank God, salvation does not depend upon how smart we are, or the knowledge we have accumulated.

MEANINGFUL WORSHIP AND A GROWING CONGREGATION

If we were to offer a miracle every Sunday, our churches would be packed to overflowing. The fact is we do have a miracle every Sunday, and every day of the week for that matter! However, we don't have miracles, by our own definition, at every worship service. We want something spectacular to take place as we worship. We want immediate healings to take place right before our eyes, as witnessed on Oral Roberts programs, and as Benny Hinn does on television today.

A miracle is an act of God which surpasses all human and natural powers. Life is a miracle. Our bodies, and the way they function is a miracle. Everything is a miracle. We aren't the ones who are in control, even though we would like to be, and think we are sometimes. When a parking space suddenly becomes available, I like to call that a *God thing* . . . others may call it a *coincidence* . . . yet others may call it a *miracle*. Whatever . . . God is in control, and He knows what is best for us at any given moment. Miracles happen every day of our lives!

We belong to God. What a great miracle that is when you consider how unfaithful we are, and yet the Lord still loves us. You are not your own, you have been bought with a price: redeemed through the blood of Christ. We so easily sing "I'm so glad that I am a part of the family of God." After you study Ephesians, you don't just want to sing it, you want to find a hill someplace and shout to the world, "I'm so glad I am a part of the family of God!" Remember, all of the words of Paul are written within the backdrop of cult worship.

"I'm so glad I'm a part of the Family of God, I've been washed in the fountain, cleansed by His Blood! Joint heirs with Jesus as we travel this sod, For I'm part of the family, The Family of God."

Being in the family of God is not our doing. It is all a matter *grace* (unmerited favor). We must always rely on God for tomorrow. In fact we do not even belong to ourselves. This should keep us humble and joyful, as part of the family of God. Our problem is that we often act like a dysfunctional family. Humbly confess that our plans may be premature.

James 4:14 *"Why, you do not even know what will happen tomorrow. What is your life? You are a mist that appears for a little while and then vanishes."*

I Corinthians 6:19 *"Do you not know that your body is a temple of the Holy Spirit, who is in you, whom you have received from God? You are not your own; 20 you were bought at a price. Therefore honor God with your body."*

The miracle we would so like to see in our day, is renewal and growth in the churches. We want people to ask "What must I do to be saved?" This will not happen as long as churches compromise the truth, or the Word of God, in order to be people pleasers. We have brought the world into the church, and have softened the Gospel, so as not to hurt anyone's feelings.

Mega churches are thriving, but not because they offer what the younger generation wants. More than likely, they are giving young parents *what they need*, and not what they want. All ages are under construction. We all have much to learn about God and His plan of salvation at any age!

Churches thrive when young parents bring their children to the church, and when the family worships together! Far too many young people are un-churched and unfamiliar with Scripture. Many adults are in the same situation. We have program after program, and the end result is that nothing concrete and lasting happens when the programs end.

Our churches have become like theaters, with large screens and sound equipment, and as much technology as can afforded; to make our worship more meaningful and pleasant. We are of the opinion we need all this to aid us in worship, and hopefully bring the younger generation and others to worship on Sundays; as well as, to make worship more meaningful and easy. There isn't anything wrong with electronic equipment. It can be a blessing if used properly for worship.

In many churches you see people worshiping the Lord with the same fervor they exhibit at a sporting event, or what has been on some of the evangelistic television broadcasts. This may be entertainment, and we have plenty of that without bringing it into the church as we worship! If we exhibit all the outward signs of enthusiasm and excitement of the entertainment world in our worship, does this mean we have finally come to the meaning of true worship? Not at all!

Is this what is happening within the mega churches? It seems to be human nature to want to be part of the new, and where the action is! But wait a minute! We have visited a few mega churches, and they are filled with sound Christian people, and the message they hear is truly very informative and inspirational: within the bounds of Scripture. Why are the people flocking to these churches? Hopefully, they are coming to worship, not because of the contemporary sounds, and all the electronic benefits at their disposal! The people are coming to some of these churches, because they are being fed with the Word of God, and encouraged to go out into the world and witness to their faith. We cannot all be mega churches, and not all mega churches are doing everything right either! Sometimes we feel a sense of hopelessness, as we try to do the best we can with what we have. Remember:

When you think there is no hope . . . there is!

When you think you have all the answers . . . you don't!

Remember **Proverbs: 16:9** *"In his heart a man plans his course, but the LORD determines his steps."* NIV

Take heart, as they say, because whatever it is that we do at worship and in life; whatever it is that we plan; know that the Lord is directing our path . . . steps. We are not as self sufficient as we think we are—i.e., in control with all the answers! It is God Who is in control. Let **James 4:15** be a starting point for understanding. Regarding our planning of things to do this passage says *"For we ought to say, "If the Lord be willing, we shall live, and do this, or that'. But you rejoice in your boastings: and all such rejoicing is evil."*

It is true . . . we quite often do not know what is best for ourselves. Whatever plans we make are mostly *our* plans . . . but it is the Lord determines the true steps of Man. It is God who determines where we will be later today or even tomorrow. Some refer to this as *a* **God thing** and it certainly is.

With all these considerations, hopefully you will be encouraged to give serious thought to what the worship of the Lord God really is. Worship is an Art, in that the individual has come to trust the Lord's directives. God is leading you to *higher ground* for that which will bless your lives, and grant you true joy, peace, and contentment. Philippians 4:5-8 *"Let your moderation be known unto all men. The Lord is at hand. 6 Be careful for nothing; but in every thing by prayer and supplication with thanksgiving let your requests be made known unto God. 7 And the peace of God, which passeth all (human) understanding, shall keep your hearts and minds through Christ Jesus. 8 Finally, brethren, whatsoever things are true, whatsoever things are honest, whatsoever things are just, whatsoever things are pure, whatsoever things are lovely, whatsoever things are of good report; if there be any virtue, and if there be any praise, think on these things."*

WE SHALL SURVIVE!

We have taken Christ out of Christmas. Our business establishments encourage their clerks to wish the customers a 'happy holiday' instead of 'merry Christmas.' The Easter Bunny and candy eggs have taken over the true meaning of Easter, that is: the celebration of Christ's resurrection. Thanksgiving has become 'turkey day.' And football has become the national god on that day. Are we saddened by what took place on what we call Good Friday? What is good about it some ask? Good Friday tells us to what extent God would go, in His determination, to fulfill His plan to save our sinful souls. Christ died for each of us as the Lamb of God, Who takes away our sin. That is a **good** thing for us! The Art part of worship comes into play when the individual willingly 'separates self' from doing what friends and others are doing. This enables the follower of Christ to dethrone self, in total surrender to God and the guidance of the Holy Spirit.

When are we going to say—"I or We've had enough?" Let's stop playing games with the worship of the Lord! The worship of the Lord God on *The Lord's Day* should take precedence over all else; football, baseball, running in competition, or all the other activities and plans with which we get involved. Oh yes: "Jesus calls us o're the tumult of *our life's wild, restless sea.*"

We know we have allowed, and therefore made possible, the tumult of today's lost society!

> *Jesus calls us o'er the tumult*
> *o*f our life's wild, restless sea;
> day by day his sweet voice soundeth,
> saying, "Christian, follow me!"

This means we need to surrender ourselves to that which is of utmost importance: As **Matthew 6:33** reads *"But seek ye first the* *kingdom of God, and his righteousness; and all these things shall be added unto you."* KJV

We have finally gotten to the point where we have put the cart before the horse; i.e., we are running ahead of God! God's Kingdom must come first in our lives: before anything else! Our desires, and what we call necessities, have been placed ahead of God's will. We want to be in control, but we are non-the-less, at all times subject to the will of God. This is what Adam and Eve failed to realize! They thought they had everything under control in that beautiful garden.

We now know what the sin of Adam and Eve has done to all of us, however we cannot blame them. We are all sinners, having made the same bad choices Adam and Eve did. For now: God has placed us on this earth, as humans, for a time of testing: to weed out those who will follow God from those who will not. Joshua has given us an example of the one great choice we must make in this life. He put it plainly before the children of Israel: **Joshua 24:15** *"Choose you this day whom ye will serve; whether the gods which your fathers served that were on the other side of the flood, or the gods of the Amorites, in whose land ye dwell: but as for me and my house, we will serve the LORD."*

Those who will not choose the Lord, shall be thrown into the lake of fire. **Revelation 20:12-14** *"And I saw the dead, great and small, standing before the throne, and books were opened. Another book was opened, which is the book of life. The dead were judged according to what they had done as recorded in the books. 13 The sea gave up the dead that were in it, and death and Hades gave up the dead that were in them, and each person was judged according to what they had done. 14 Then death and Hades were thrown into the lake of fire. The lake of fire is the second death."*

The Word of God gives us a way out of this problem, as revealed in the Bible, and through His Holy Spirit. It takes time to learn what the Bible teaches. Remember the hymn:

Take time to be holy,
speak oft with thy Lord;
abide in him always,
and feed on his word.
Make friends of God's children,
help those who are weak,
forgetting in nothing
his blessing to seek.

These words are redemptive, if one is fully aware of their meaning. Take time to be set apart from the world. We are in the world: not of it. It is not about us, it is all about God who is calling to His people through every experience of life. Therefore, the Art of it is simply learning to place one's trust in God, above all else. Learn to listen for God is speaking! His Holy Spirit convicts all of us of sin, without exception, for we are sinners! The art of it comes into play as we practice yielding to God daily, and this necessitates the prioritizing our time, so regular corporate worship will be the norm, and not something we decided upon each Sunday. We need to discipline ourselves to the reading and studying the Manual for Life (The Holy Scripture), accompanied by prayer, and living a prayerful life daily, and helping others in need! This is not easy with all our many worldly interests! So much to do and so little time to do it!

The words of Jesus often *step on our toes*. This is what worship does for us: it gives us opportunity to *Praise God from Who All Blessings Flow*, while at the same time, to know this is an opportunity to repent, grow, and respond to the Lord. True worship enables the individual to go out into the world as an inspired, uplifted, and forgiven sinner, seeking to serve Christ. What other choice do we have? Thank God for the one choice we do have—to serve Jesus Christ, the Son of the Living God, our personal Savior! **It is so easy to neglect such service in this fast paced society! We also know there are many who do not want to hear the truth: not even from Jesus. At one point, Jesus had** been teaching in the Synagogue, and the Scripture coming up next informs us that not everyone responded to the teachings of Jesus.!

John 6:60-70 *On hearing it (the words of Jesus in the Synagogue on this occasion), many of his disciples said, "This is a hard teaching. Who can accept it?"* 61 *Aware that his disciples were grumbling about this, Jesus said to them, "Does this offend you?* 62 *What if you see the Son of Man ascend to where he was before!* 63 *The Spirit gives life; the flesh counts for nothing. The words I have spoken to you are spirit and they are life.* 64 *Yet there are some of you who do not believe." For Jesus had known from the beginning which of them did not believe and who would betray him.* 65 *He went on to say, "This is why I told you that no one can come to me unless the Father has enabled him."* 66 *From this time many of his disciples (follovrs) turned back and no longer followed him.* 67 *"You do not want to leave too, do you?" Jesus asked the Twelve.* 68 *Simon Peter answered him, "Lord, to whom shall we go? You have the words of eternal life.* 69 *We believe and know that you are the Holy One of God."* 70 *Then Jesus replied, "Have I not chosen you, the Twelve? Yet one of you is a devil!"* KJV

What about verse 65 above? *"This is why I told you that no one can come to me unless the Father has enabled him."* About all we can say at this point is what the disciples said in verse **60** *"This is a hard teaching. Who can accept it?"* The words of Jesus in the Synagogue were truth, but we humans do not always want the truth! The saving grace of this passage are the words of Simon Peter who said to Jesus, *"Lord, to whom shall we go? You have the words of eternal life. We believe and know that you are the Holy one of God."* These should be our words as well. **Acts 4:12 reads:** *"Neither is there salvation in any other: for there is none other name under heaven given among men, whereby we must be saved."*

ARE WE FICKLE OR JUST CARELESS?

We have all had the experience of liking someone, and then for some reason, after a time, this *like* turned into *dislike*. The opposite is also true. We may not like and individual until we come to really know that person, then that dislike turns into a friendship. In the same way, many individuals make contact with God, and look upon Him and His Church favorably. They feel the need to worship Him on The Lords Day and then, after a time, for some unknown reason this feeling does not last. Individuals may start coming to corporate worship with good intentions. Some may even get involved in the life of the church, then suddenly for no apparent reason they disappear, and are apparently no longer interested in the church: from all outward appearances. Are these persons just fickle or careless? No doubt they are sincere . . . sincerely wrong!

II **Timothy 3:7** speaks of individuals who are *"ever learning, and never able to come to the knowledge of the truth."*

This is a very sad situation: ever learning, but not able to come to the truth.

WARNING—**Hebrews 6:4** *"For it is impossible for those who were once enlightened, and have tasted of the heavenly gift, and were made partakers of the Holy Ghost, 5 And have tasted the good word of God, and the powers of the world to come, 6 If they shall fall away, to renew them again unto repentance; seeing they crucify to themselves the Son of God afresh, and put him to an open shame.*

True worship is serious business! Worship is not a program designed for entertainment. There is a huge difference between being inspired, which leads to motivation for service, and entertainment, that gives one a temporary high.

Now that we have seen Mankind as fallen a creature, who has made a mess of things on earth, let us turn our attention to the mix-up and confusion we have made in the corporate worship of Almighty God.

Once we understand the importance of **worshiping in Spirit and in truth**; our top and next priority, is to choose a church that is built upon **Biblical Worship**. When many people decide go to church, they often choose a church for the wrong reason. For example: my friends and business contacts go to that church; it's the closest church to our home: the church has a good youth program; the worship service is fun and exciting; and the pastor tells great jokes. **Biblical worship and Scriptural preaching must take priority over all else.** The local church is not a social club. It is a place where God's people worship and experience fellowship. Our worship must honor God.

STEWARDSHIP

God has given all of us **specific talents**, no matter how humble they may be. It is important to cultivate whatever talent the Lord has given. It is vital to connect with what Jesus is saying in **Matthew 25:14-29** *"Again, it will be like a man going on a journey, who called his servants and entrusted his property to them. 15 To one he gave five talents of money, to another two talents, and to another one talent, each according to his ability. Then he went on his journey. 16 The man who had received the five talents went at once and put his money to work and gained five more. 17 So also, the one with the two talents gained two more. 18 But the man who had received the one talent went off, dug a hole in the ground and hid his master's money. 19 After a long time the master of those servants returned and settled accounts with them. 20 The man who had received the five talents brought the other five. 'Master,' he said, 'you entrusted me with five talents. See, I have gained five more.' 21 His lord said unto him, Well done, thou good and faithful servant: thou hast been faithful over a few things, I will make thee ruler over many things: enter thou into the joy of thy lord. 22 He also that had received two talents came and said, 'Lord, thou deliveredst unto me two talents: behold, I have gained two other talents beside them.' 23 His lord said unto him, Well done, good and faithful servant; thou hast been faithful* *over a few things, I will make* **thee** *ruler over many things: enter thou into the joy of thy lord.* **24** *Then he which had received the one talent came and said, Lord, 'I knew thee that thou art an hard man, reaping where thou hast not sown, and gathering where thou hast not strawed;* **25** *And I was afraid, and went and hid thy talent in the earth: lo, there thou hast that is thine.'* **26** *His lord answered and said unto him, Thou wicked and slothful servant, thou knewest that I reap where I sowed not, and gather where I have not strawed:* **27** *Thou oughtest therefore to have put my money to the exchangers, and then at my coming I should have received mine own with usury.* **28** *Take therefore the talent from him, and give it unto him which hath ten talents.* **29** *For unto every one that hath shall be given, and he shall have abundance : but from him that hath not shall be taken away even that which he hath.* **30** *And cast ye the unprofitable servant into outer darkness: there shall be weeping and gnashing of teeth."*

In this parable our Lord is obviously talking about money? Tithing involves money, and all our resources, which by the way belong to God, not to you or me! Tithing is for the benefit of the people of God. God doesn't need our money: it is already His . . . He owns everything, and is creator of all! It is important that church members understand that we all are a part of what God is doing: He is still creating! The Bible speaks about the giving of our *first fruits* (not the leftovers). God has promised He will bless us beyond our wildest dreams. Tithing is one of the most powerful disciplines a Christian can practice to get his or her finances and life in line with God's will. Indeed, it is a Biblical mandate. **Malachi 3:10** *"Bring ye all the tithes into the storehouse, that there may be meat in mine house, and prove me now herewith, saith the LORD of hosts, if I will not open you the windows of heaven and pour you out a blessing, that there shall not be room enough to receive it."* KJV

The offering, during corporate worship, is the high point in one's experience at worship. The reason being, we are not only supporting the Lord's work through the giving of a check or cash into the collection plate, we are, at the same time, giving or yielding ourselves unto the Lord in a concrete manner. God paid a huge price to redeem us from sin! Now it is out turn to give as we are able to the Lord. Everything is the Lord's anyway!

This is why we sometimes sing, after the offering is taken, "All things come of Thee, O Lord, and of Thine own have we given Thee." Everything you think is yours really belongs to God, even you belong to God! **I Corinthians 6:19** *"Do you not know that your body is a temple of the Holy Spirit, who is in you, whom you have received from God? You are not your own; 20 you were bought at a price. Therefore honor God with your body."*

ARE WE SNOBS?

David Garvin, a Duke Divinity School student says: "I admit, I am guilty of worship snobbery, and a liturgical snob."

"Give me a well-put together service of worship, a theologically sound and intellectually challenging sermon, and a choir second only to the heavenly chorus."

"I fear that I am not alone. When one enters into different churches the demographics and homogeneity (similar in kind or nature) of various worship services are predictable. Younger people, including some middle aged individuals congregate with their age group at 'contemporary' worship services. Those who have always worshiped in a traditional manner gather to worship 'traditionally.' Different styles of worship and worships rarely mix."

"WHEN OUR ALLEGIANCE TO A PARTICULAR WORSHIP STYLE OVERSHADOWS OUR ALLEGIANCE TO THE ONE WORSHIPED, WE'VE MISSED THE POINT! WORSHIP BECOMES OUR IDOL; WE BOW DOWN TO THE PRESENTATION OF THE MORTAL OVER THE IMMORTAL. OUR EMOTIONAL

AND PSYCHOLOGICAL NEEDS—NOT OUR NEED TO PRAISE
AND GLORIFY GOD—TAKE CENTER STAGE."

The corporate worship experience is needed but for one purpose: to praise God, the Creator of all that exists. **Psalm 19:1-6** *"The heavens declare the glory of God; and the firmament sheweth his handywork. 2 Day unto day uttereth speech, and night unto night sheweth knowledge. 3 There is no speech nor language, where their voice is not heard. 4 Their line is gone out through all the earth, and their words to the end of the world. In them hath he set a tabernacle for the sun, 5 Which is as a bridegroom coming out of his chamber, and rejoiceth as a strong man to run a race. 6 His going forth is from the end of the heaven, and his circuit unto the ends of it: and there is nothing hid from the heat thereof."* KJV

Listen to the Psalmist: **Psalm 27:4** *"One thing have I desired of the LORD, that will I seek after; that I may dwell in the house of the LORD all the days of my life, to behold the beauty of the LORD, and to enquire in his temple."* KJV

"Worship is not bowing down to our own preferences, and loosing ourselves in our own worshipful delights. Rather, true worship is getting lost in the wonder love and praise of God, Who calls and invites us to enter His holy and mysterious presence always, everywhere, and in any manner." (Taken from The *United Methodist Reporter*) David Garvin serves as pastor of Shiloh United Methodist Church in Liberty, N.C.)

So our worship must always be carefully scrutinized, and be given first priority in life, because without God, we are nothing! Worship is an Art in that it is always being refined, renewed, and beautified, to the end that the worshiper is inspired and motivated. What can we do better in the future from what we are doing now, or have done in the past? Neither contemporary nor traditional worship has reached what it should be, because both have become self-centered, self seeking, and self satisfied! When worshiping, it is so necessary that we *dethrone self* as we worship and give God His rightful place!

Regardless of how the individual worships the Lord in the corporate worship setting, the main thing to ask is this, "Is my style of worship acceptable to God?" Humans are not the judge: God is. It is God to Whom we must answer! The Word of God is soundly dogmatic in its assessment of the way God's children should behave at corporate worship and outside the church building as well. If there is a problem, we can change even though we remain sinners who make mistakes. We are God's forgiven and forgiving children *Under Construction*. None of us have arrived at perfection! We would like to think we have arrived, but this is part of being human, fallen creatures of the Lord. However, God has fixed that! He has already weighed in on our problem, and has fixed our situation through His Son! God wants to give us eternal life in His presence!

EVERYONE HAS FAITH

What is this faith everyone has? It is simple if you stop to think about it. Whether we realize it or not, we all live by faith. People have faith in their automobile brakes! We have faith that the lights will go on when we enter a room and flip the switch. We have faith that Wal-Mart will be open when we want to go shopping. If the doctor tells you to take a certain pill and it will help you feel better; you take the pill. We all have this kind of faith! Why is it so difficult to have faith in God? The problem isn't that we don't have faith, because we all have it. Where we place this faith of ours is what really matters! Our problem exists when we place faith in everything God has given us, and have forgotten about God! **Matthew 6:33** speaks to this need: *"But seek ye first the kingdom of God, and his righteousness; and all these things shall be added unto you."* KJV And **Romans 1:25** tells it like it is: *"We changed the truth of God into a lie, and worshipped and served the creature more than the Creator, who is blessed for ever. Amen."*
We all need to see to it that our faith is well placed!

Look at Creation, and you will see God's handiwork! We cannot help but see it! At the same time, however, it is all together too easy to worship God's creation, and in the process forget the Creator! **Romans 1:25** *"Man has changed the truth of God into a lie, and worshipped and served the creature more than the Creator, who is blessed for ever. Amen."* KJV

From where does our faith come? Many individuals want to have faith in God, but it seems to be out of their reach! It is faith placed in Jesus Christ that grants eternal life, it is a *gift from God*, and anyone may have it, but not everyone will get it, because we want to be in control! Being in control takes time. The end result is we run out of time, and have no time to take God seriously.

FAITH IS REVEALED IN SCRIPTURE

Hebrews 11:1 *"Now faith is being sure of what we hope for and certain of what we do not see."* NIV

Hebrews 11:1 *"Now faith is the substance of things hoped for, the evidence of things not seen."* KJV

Hebrews 11:1 *"To have faith is to be sure of the things we hope for, to be certain of the things we cannot see."* GNT (Good News Translation)

Hebrews 11:1 *"What is faith? It is the confident assurance that what we hope for is going to happen. It is the evidence of things we cannot yet see."* NLB (New Living Bible)

Hebrews 11:1 *"Now faith is the assurance of things hoped for, the conviction of things not seen."* RSV

Concentrate on the various versions and translations noted above.

Everything must die to be changed. A seed must be planted, then die unto itself in order that it may grow and produce new life. Faith gives the assurance we all need, in this temporary state in which we live. When we see an object, we know it is there, and this does not require faith. However *reality is made up of much more than those things we can see and touch!*

I shall always appreciate one of the scenes from the old movie "One Foot in Heaven," where Pastor Spence goes into the pharmacy to visit the pharmacist. While there his dentist walks into the drug store for one of those good old fashioned sodas. He invites pastor Spence to have a soda with him at the counter. While visiting, the discussion turned to the human soul. The dentist asks pastor Spence if he could prove he has a soul. The dentist's argument goes as follows: "So you think you have a soul . . . can you feel it; can you touch it; can you see it; can you taste it; can you smell it; can you hear it?" To each of these questions pastor Spence answers, "No". The dentist responds dogmatically, "Then your senses are against you: you don't have a soul."

Now it is pastor Spence's turn. He asks the dentist, "Have you ever had a tooth ache? Can you touch it; can you see it; can you taste it; can you smell it; can you hear it?" The friendly dentist answers, "No." Then the pastor gives an answer worthy of Socrates himself: "Then my friend, your senses are against you . . . you've never had a tooth ache."

We've been reading about faith. Now we turn to the source of the kind of **faith** that really matters . . . <u>*Saving faith*</u> is a gift from God!

"Wesley believed that the living core of the Christian faith was revealed in **Scripture**, illumined by **tradition**, vivified in personal **experience**, and confirmed by **reason**. Scripture [however] is primary, revealing the Word of God so far as it is necessary for our salvation."

Scripture—*the Holy Bible (Old and New Testaments)*
Tradition—*the two millennia history of the Christian Church*
Reason—*rational thinking and sensible interpretation*
Experience—*a Christian's personal and communal journey in Christ*

When an individual is ordained for ministry, at least in the United Methodist Church, he or she is asked "Will you move on to perfection?" We better answer "Yes."

What is perfection? Paul admonishes us to go on to perfection, but is that possible? We often reason away our imperfections with the rationale, "Well, I'm only human, not perfect: no one is! We have lots of company."

Armed with these ready phrases we can go through life ignoring, and not squarely facing, or even knowing of Paul's instruction: "That we go on perfection (maturity the faith). (**Hebrews 6:1**) _Therefore let us leave the elementary teachings about Christ and go on to maturity, not laying again the foundation of repentance from acts that lead to death, and of faith in God,"_ NIV

On judgment day, Jesus will be dividing the sheep from the goats. Moving on to maturity (or _going on to perfection_), we must keep growing, learning and moving on to higher levels of the Christian faith and experience. We are always in the construction process, until we finally realize that what we do to the least individual, we are also doing it to Christ.

Matthew 25:31-40 gives us words to carefully consider: **31** *"When the Son of man shall come in his glory, and all the holy angels with him, then shall he sit upon the throne of his glory: 32 And before him shall be gathered all nations: and he shall separate them one from another, as a shepherd divideth his sheep from the goats: 33 And he shall set the sheep on his right hand, but the goats on the left. 34 Then shall the King say unto them on his right hand, Come, ye blessed of my Father, inherit the kingdom prepared for you from the foundation of the world: 35 For I was an hungred, and ye gave me meat: I was thirsty, and ye gave me drink: I was a stranger, and ye took me in: 36 Naked, and ye clothed me: I was sick, and ye visited me: I was in prison, and ye came unto me. 37 Then shall the righteous answer him, saying, Lord, when saw we thee an hungered, and fed thee? or thirsty, and gave thee drink? 38 When saw we thee a stranger, and took thee in? or naked, and clothed thee? 39 Or when saw we thee sick, or in prison, and came unto thee? 40 And the King shall answer and say* *unto them, Verily I say unto you, Inasmuch as ye have done it unto one of the least of these my brethren, ye have done it unto me." KJV*

MUSIC IN OUR LIVES

"Music is part of our history. It is an expression of who we are and the times we've known: Our highs and our lows . . . and so much that we love. Take away American music from the American story and you take away a good part of the soul of the story. It is impossible to imagine life in America without it . . . without Shenandoah, Amazing Grace, Over the Rainbow, or Okalahoma, The Battle Hymn of the Republic or America the Beautiful, or the music of Christmas in America." (Taken from *"In the Dark Streets Shineth"* as narrated by David McCullough, with the Mormon Tabernacle Choir.)

Because music has such a profound affect or influence upon individuals, it has been said that *music sooths the savage beast in us*. However, it can also be said that some music brings out the beast in us. This depends upon the kind of music to which a person may be listening at a given time.

If you are serious and honest about worship; you must first look at what music is, and how it has evolved through the years. If you do this, you will soon learn that the great music has not changed for centuries. Richard Wagner's music, composed in the 1800's, is still very popular; as is Tchaikovsky's music; and in the 1700's there is the music of Mozart, Beethoven, and Bach. And the list continues. Symphony Hall on satellite Radio proudly announces they play music from the past 1000 years, and they can do this, because the classics are timeless. The sounds of later and more contemporary composers such as Igor Stravinsky, Prokofiev, Copland and Shostakovich, were quite different from their earlier colleagues. Great music is still great music, and this includes classical, opera, country, and some of the big bands and even jazz if you can understand it. Jokingly, I say of Jazz, "When they find out where they are going, then I will listen." Remember, music must conform to its definition. (See Page 126 ff).

MUSIC IN THE CHURCH

Music has always played a central role in worship. Some churches are large enough to afford a '*Minister of Music.*' This individual should be trained in the art of knowing what lends itself to true worship. Again it cannot be over-emphasized, that *music does sooth the savage beast in all of us*. Music used for worship services touch our lives in a way that the spoken word can't. Make certain that music used for worship is in keeping with the Word of God (theologically correct).

FAMOUS QUOTATIONS ABOUT MUSIC

Listed are a few examples of how music has touched the lives of some people:

"Music expresses that which cannot be said and on which it is impossible to remain silent." ;Victor Hugo)
"Music is the voice of the soul." Author Unknown
If a composer could say what he had to say in words he would not bother trying to say it in music. ~Gustav Mahler
There is nothing in the world so much like prayer as music is. ~William P. Merrill
My idea is that there is music in the air, music all around us; the world is full of it, and you simply take as much as you require. ~Edward Elgar
Life can't be all bad when for ten dollars you can buy all the Beethoven sonatas and listen to them for ten years. ~William F. Buckley, Jr.
[An intellectual] is someone who can listen to the "William Tell Overture" without thinking of the Lone Ranger. ~John Chesson
Music is the universal language of mankind. ~Henry Wadsworth Longfellow

Music is the shorthand of emotion. ~Leo Tolstoy
The joy of music should never be interrupted by a commercial. ~Leonard Bernstein
(Taken off the Internet)

INSPIRATION/MOTIVATION/ACTION

My wife and I listen to The Hour of Power every Saturday night. Most of the time you will hear a great and challenging message, that will inspire you to walk more faithfully with the Lord.

The Great inspirational music heard on The Hour of Power for 40+ years had suddenly had been turned over to a contemporary format with a praise team. The Hour of Power, that Robert Schuller had founded, was now totally contemporary, with the exception of the fine messages, given by Sheila (Robert Schuller's daughter). At that time, the magnificent organ stood idle. The audience was not shown, because it had become so sparse. The *praise team* looked as though they were auditioning for a part in a movie. The choir director gave the impression he was doing exercises at a gym: his arms were stretched out everywhere. During this contemporary phase, the great hymn of testimony: *"It is Well with My Soul,"* was sung to a strong rock beat. The soloist exhibited several physical and facial contortions, as she swayed back and forth: putting the mike against her lips. No doubt she was of the opinion that she was demonstrating her deep faith for all to see. Yet it looked so programmatic, artificial, hypocritical or fake, that it gave the impression that she had no idea of how this great music should be sung, or how it came to be written. This totally destroyed the inspiration behind such a great hymn, and it left one feeling empty, disappointed, and a bit upset: having been cheated out of what could have been a tremendous source of inspiration.

The artist is never more important than the music used. You may say "Hey! The music inspired me!" Of course it did; much like the inspiration one feels when doing what everyone else is doing at a given moment. One person stands, and then everyone stands. One person claps then everyone claps. When you walk down the street sometime, start looking up at the sky. You will note that everyone is looking up to see what you may or may not be seeing. We are joiners in many areas of group or individual behavior.

Something had to be done because of the Crystal Cathedral's financial problems. With the new contemporary format, the magnificent organ stood silent, the choir was no longer present, and the audience was on longer scanned for all to see because it had become so sparse. In its place stood the praise team. This did not bring about the newness and growth which was so needed, and which they had hoped would help the financially stressed Hour of Power in its time of need. When Sheila quit the program, they began showing reruns of their former broadcasts.

After a few weeks of showing reruns of their glorious past, we are so thankful, The Hour of Power is back alive and well. The magnificent organ is once again heard, the choir is back, and the audience is now scanned and the Crystal Cathedral is filled once again. The Crystal Cathedral has been sold to the Roman Catholic Church. Soon (as of this writing) an announcement will be made to inform us where The Hour of Power services will be held. Robert Schuller's grandson Bobby, is, as of now, leader and is doing an excellent job and has been giving very inspirational messages.

As we worship today in our churches, is it possible to be worshiping self and one's surroundings, instead of God. Malachi steps down very hard on those of his day, who considered themselves to be worshiping and praising God, while their personal lives and motives were not pleasing to the Lord. **Malachi 1:10** *"Oh, that one of you would shut the temple doors, so that you would not light useless fires on my altar! I am not pleased with you," says the LORD Almighty, "and I will accept no offering from your hands."* NIV

Amos 5:21-23 *"I hate, I despise your religious feasts; I cannot stand your assemblies.* **22** *Even though you bring me burnt offerings and grain offerings, I will not accept them. Though you bring choice fellowship offerings, I will have no regard for them.* **23** *Away with the noise of your songs! I will not listen to the music of your harps.*

When we worship the Lord God, it must be done in the spirit of humble selflessness, coupled with the awareness of personal sin, and not pride in who we are, and where we are in the faith! We have not arrived where we should be as the children of God, so we should not act like it in our worship! We are always growing in the Christian walk. It is a journey, so we need to keep ourselves humble, and not act as though we had arrived at *perfection*. What we really are is forgiven and forgiving sinners in need of God's grace. If one approaches God as did Isaiah when he entered the House of the Lord, there will be no room for boredom as one worships. Because of God's grace (unmerited favor), we must totally rely upon God as did Isaiah. (See Isaiah's Call, page 40)

Sad to say, but true, many consider traditional worship to be boring, and it can be, if we come into the Lord's house for reasons other than for *Biblical Worship, seeing God high and lifted up.* We should be meditating, and praying before the corporate worship service begins. Our prayer should be *"God, what are you up to today?"* Quite often, when we come to worship, we get it backwards. We say *"God, this is what I am up to today, and I want you to be a part of it and bless it. I want you to hear my prayers and bless me. I will worship my way, but I still want Your blessings Lord."* In today's confused world, compromises only *appear* to be working! The attitude of many is, 'Lord bless, whatever it is we are doing at worship, so all ages will want to come to church. And Lord; I want You to bless our worship! I want You Lord, to make our church grow, but I want it to be done on my terms, and in keeping with what I do and like!' This is akin to praying amiss. It is too filled with "I, me, and my." **Thy** will be done Lord!

Why do we concentrate so heavily upon getting young people into our churches? The answer is this—because there is an overwhelmingly number of elderly persons at worship and we want and need young people if the Church is going to continue being the church. All ages need the church. We are experiencing an apostasy (a falling away) in our congregations today. We would like to find an answer as to why this is happening? **II Thessalonians 2;3** reads: *"Let no man deceive you by any means: for that day shall not come, except there come a falling away first, and that man of sin be revealed, the son of perdition;* KJV or—" *Let no one deceive you by any means; for that Day will not come unless the falling away comes first, and the man of sin is revealed, the son of perdition,* NKJV

That Day refers to the second coming of the Lord.

In seminary, one of our professors was an excellent magician. The young people loved him. I have seen him do what seems to be the impossible. Then one day, by the grace of God, he felt this magic act performance had taken over his life. He promised the Lord he would give it all up, and become a dedicated minister of the Lord. This he did, but surprisingly as it was to him, after becoming God's faithful servant, God gave his magic abilities back to him, now to be used once in a while to God's glory. He now did this to the glory of God, and not for personal gratification as a celebrity.

The emerging church is determined to bring today's sounds and rhythms into the church. What is seen and heard in many churches now, is geared toward showmanship and entertainment. The tapping of feet, the waving of arms, and swaying from side to side, is not worship, it is a demonstration. Such additions, called worship, may be likened to an *ego high* or *self worship*, and it is done to let others in the congregation see how Christian and dedicated the individual is, although no one would ever admit to this.

The organ has been likened to the voice of God. If this is true, we may be guilty *turning off the voice of God*; and, have instead turned on the *praise band, and song leader/s* as they take center stage. What has happened to our humility and standing in awe at the grace and presence of God? What has happened to **Biblical preaching; The** *call to Repentance; Inspiration; The Trinity; The Second Coming of Christ, Justification; Sanctification; The devil; the Virgin Birth; and The Wrath of God (in other words, God's word in total and our response to it?)*

When we come before God in worship, we come as forgiven and forgiving sinners by the grace of God. This fact alone should be enough to profoundly humble the worshiper. We are somewhat aware of what God has done for us, but is this enough? Worshipers *desperately* need the inspiration of God's Word, to face with hope, what is ahead of them with encouragement. Being *entertained* and being *inspired* are two different happenings. *Inspiration* leads to *Motivation* and *motivation leads to a life of action as we serve the Lord!* Entertainment makes us **feel good,** but that feeling is soon dissipated and forgotten. The emerging church, with its inadequate methods of worship, is very subtly creeping into the worship of God in our churches. Come just as you are . . . forget about formality and preparations. Hang loose, as they say in Hawaii. (See Dressing Appropriately For Worship, page 198) How does our worship match up with **Psalm 51:17** *"The sacrifices of God are a broken spirit; a broken and contrite heart, O God, you will not despise."* NIV

We habitually come into the worship experience displaying our pride, joy, and boldness. True, Scripture speaks of **boldness**, but when we come before the Lord with boldness . . . it is not because we have earned that right through our personal righteousness. We can come before the Lord boldly, only because of what Christ has done for us. And remember the world's definition of boldness may not be ours. We usually think a person is bold if he or she is brave, daring, flashy, and outgoing to the point of knowing it all, etc. I like to think of boldness as coming before the Lord feeling unworthy, humble, repentant, and willing to hear the Word of the Lord. **Ephesians 3:12** reads: *"In whom (Jesus) we have boldness and access with confidence by the faith of him."* KJV And in **Hebrews 10:17-19** we read: *"And their sins and iniquities will I remember no more.* **18** *"Now where remission of these* *is, there is no more offering for sin. 19 Having therefore, brethren, boldness to enter into the holiest by the blood of Jesus . . ."* KJV

Only through Christ we may have boldness to approach God. However, we all need to quiet down and know that God is present, as He has promised. Sanctuaries should inspire quietness. Walk into a Roman Catholic Church, or an Episcopal church, and the very atmosphere causes us to whisper ever so slightly. Why . . . because we sense we are on holy ground; and in the presence of God! This is a holy place.

When we enter a mortuary for visitation, we quiet down, sensing the importance of why we are present . . . out of respect, and to be of comfort to the grieving family. Can we not respect the Lord as much? He created us . . . has given us life, along with the beauty of the earth; even the air we breathe . . . and, has provided a way for our sin to be forgiven and forgotten! If this doesn't humble us and quiet down our spirits, then nothing really can! The world isn't going to quiet us down!

WHAT HAS HAPPENED TO MUSIC

I used to make fun of classical music, because it was so foreign to me as a teenager. It was through exposure to such compositions and arrangements, that I grew to appreciate the big band, country, classical and sacred music. The Big Bands disappeared, we are told, because people had stopped dancing. Well, hopefully by now, we know this is not true! People are still dancing. In my opinion, Glenn Miller's band was the best of the rest. But Glenn Miller had died. Other bands tried to keep their place in the sun, but were financially stressed. The Beatles and Elvis were all that was needed to bring to the world a new and different sound. Individuals and small groups were taking over the music world. The big bands began to fade away as the small groups and individuals were highly promoted, and this trend was very profitable. Overnight Elvis, and Michael became teenage idols: each a king we are told. Oh No!!! There is only one **King** and that is **Jesus the Lord**!

This list of performers continues to grow as there are endless hundreds to add to this list. The individual and small group performers, have become the fashion. People still dance, but to a different tune.

The Beatles even claimed themselves to be more popular than Jesus Christ. Elvis was the product of promoters who stood to make huge profits off his of performances. He even made some sacred CDs. Talent didn't really matter. All a person had to have was great looks, an outgoing winsome personality, and sex appeal. In the earlier days of Elvis, television cameras were not allowed to show him from the waist down, because his bodily movements were to suggestive. Elvis was told by his promoters, that it would be to his best interest to seldom smile, since his sober face and a sexy presence would arouse his female audience, even though they knew they could never have him.

When listening to bad sounds long enough, a person begins to like them, and so do their friends, especially if there are no better profitable alternatives offered. Today, comparatively speaking, most young people are not listening to jazz, sacred, country, western, big band, or symphonic music. This is not where the profits are. The great symphonic orchestras and operatic music is available, but these have to depend upon subscribers and supporters. Notice following the "Great Performances" on public television, there is a long list of foundations and individuals who make the broadcast possible. Great music is not offered as regular programming on television, because it is next to impossible to find sponsors. There is not enough money to be made. What is being shown on television apparently is what the public wants. This is a very sad and disturbing commentary on the morals of Americans, and the world in general.

We know, as we watch some of these groups on television, or in concert, that tattoos, sex and drugs go hand in hand with these sounds. The sounds of heavy metal grate upon the music lover's ears. These arrangements reflect the *tortured soul of Man* in today's world: food for thought! Let us not be guilty of blaspheme when we are dealing with the Name of Holy God, our Redeemer.

Not all sacred contemporary music is of this nature however, as some of it is very good. However, much of the contemporary music is not praise music, <u>just because we label it as such</u>. Calling it *praise music* does not make it so, any more than standing in your garage makes you a car. Such music lacks depth; is filled with repetition, and evokes bodily movement, and misses the directive of God, where He instructs in **Psalm 46 and verse 10** *"Be still and know that I am God: I will be exalted among the heathen, I will be exalted in the earth."* Read the Beatitudes in Matthew 5 as well.

Sex and drugs may have taken over the entertainment world. But no one can mingle sex and drugs with music such as Handel's Messiah: so it was thought; but. Hollywood finally found a way. Some corrupt director has allowed such blaspheme, and called it humor, in the movie, "Dumb and Dumber," where "The Hallelujah Chorus" is sung as a bus load of nearly naked young women step off a bus, and model themselves before the two very dumb men who were looking for transportation. Stand up comics take great pride in blaspheming the Lord, and in the use of filthy unseeingly dirty words; and, the audience calls this humor! Why do audiences laugh when God's Name is blasphemed along with anything that is *holy*? Such language in movies is totally unnecessary, and ruins many fine stories!

As far as symphonies are concerned, many of them were composed over 1000 years ago, and have withstood the test of time. The universal language—music, has drastically changed since the end of World War II, and we can give satan the credit! <u>The devil knows exactly how to get control of our minds</u>! By no stretch of a rational mind, can one justify the loud volume of today's rhythmic sounds, which invoke the exact same kind of frenzy as was exhibited at the foot of Mt. Sinai (see page 9 ff).

The frenzy at the foot of Mt. Sinai was orchestrated by satan, and has reared its ugly head again in today's hyper-filled entertainment! People <u>do not</u>, as in the fallacy of evolution, <u>grow progressively better</u>. If left to what we call *human nature*, the process is quite the opposite. Without careful attention, we go down hill. This is how we are: sinners to the end, but forgiven only through one's acceptance of Christ. This point need not be discussed, since we know of too many celebrities of the contemporary sounds, that have turned to the use of drugs, tattoos, filthy and obscene language, sexual immorality, false religious philosophies, and occults. They have experienced broken homes, along with divorce after divorce. **The tortured soul of Man is depicted in his music**! It should be noted that getting into the hearing aid business may be a good idea these days. **The music to which we listen is one of the first signs of moral deterioration!**

THE BIG BANDS

The big bands were **not** made up of one person in competition with others of the organization. For example . . . Glenn Miller's band, the Modernaires, and soloists (vocal or instrumental) all performed as one to create that unforgettable Miller sound. The glory did <u>not</u> go to one individual; not even the band leader, by whose name the band was known. If there were any praise given, it went too the **band in total**. The same was true of most big bands, but admittedly, some were not very good. Those who really shine yet today, as great examples of harmoniously blended music are: Glenn Miller, Harry James, Tommy Dorsey, Dick Jurgens, Sammy Kaye, Blue Barran, Kaye Keyser, Guy Lombardo, and others of this caliber. They were a *blend of the total group* to make that *one harmonious big band sound*. Most arrangements were an inspiration!

We were at Disneyland several years ago when the Harry James band was performing in an open air dance area. We stood outside the fenced section where people were dancing, just to listen and watch. While standing there, a group of teenagers came along, and for some reason they decided to stop and listen to the Harry James band. They stood there listening without speaking, when suddenly one of them said to the others in his group, "I had no idea how <u>great the big band sound is when hearing it in person!</u>" All his friends agreed! They stayed to listen longer than we did. This speaks volumes to me. Young people can really enjoy the big band sound, if they are exposed to it! Admittedly, music sounds much different when hearing it in person, as compared to listening from an electronic device or recordings, no matter how sophisticated one's sound equipment may be.

If each individual did his own thing in an orchestra, without paying attention to what others were playing, or the written music, chaos would be the result. Without years of practice and endless rehearsals, the big bands. and great orchestras of the nation could not exist.

To make great music, and to be of witness to the world, we need unity, harmony, humility, and dedication to a common goal within the Church. *Individualism destroys what the body of Christ (the Church) is seeking to accomplish. WWJD (What Would Jesus Do?)* is still a popular slogan. The problem is that it is easier to wear the band around the wrist, than to live the life. A friend of ours put it this way "Walk your talk." **Ephesians 4:4-6** *"There is one body, and one Spirit, even as ye are called in one hope of your calling; 5 One Lord, one faith, one baptism, 6 One God and Father of all, who is above all, and through all, and in you all."* Who has divided the body of Christ? We sinners did it, and are still doing it!

MUCH SECULAR MUSIC COMES FROM THE CLASSICS

Most individuals have little awareness of how the motion picture industry uses music to impact the story being told. The majority of background music in motion pictures is of the classical idiom. From the classical sounds of the score, one can tell if the scene is to be: romantic, joyful and happy, dramatic, comic, portraying impending danger, death, spooky, or of an inspirational nature, etc. Movie goers sit with their eyes glued to the action on the screen with little thought of the background music being used. Most of the time they are listening to classical music, without knowing it. Even Satellite radio has one station called 'Escape to the Movies' on XM radio channel 27. This station plays nothing but background music from the motion pictures. Sometimes the dialogue is also played. It is almost like listening to a symphony concert.

Alfred Newman, now deceased, was for much of his career, the most influential and respected composer and music director in Hollywood. Today we have John Williams, who is currently the biggest name in the history of movie music, and no doubt the most widely-heard composer of the last one hundred years. Williams began composing for television in the late 1950s, eventfully moving on to feature films in the 1960s. In 1972 he won an Oscar for his orchestration of the music for Fiddler on the Roof. In 1974 he began a long and fruitful collaboration with Steven Spielberg that would lead to some of his best known work, including the Oscar winning score to Jaws, in 1975. Williams has also been guest conductor of the Boston Pops Orchestra. His film work also includes the music for Superman, and the list continues to grow.

Great composers for the film industry are not composing background music to boost their ego, but it is profitable. They are sincerely trying to add meaning and inspiration and depth, to the scenes being depicted in story line of the film. **In the worship of God, we need to use music that will add depth, meaning and inspiration to our worship**: also, to better enable our numb spirits to see God, whom we are trying our best to worship. <u>Music hath charm to soothe the savage beast</u>. Music reaches the depth of our hearts more powerfully than the spoken word!

Thus far, I have sought to enlighten my readers about the kinds of music that, not only sets the mood for specific scenes in motion pictures, but music that is being very much appreciated by the movie goers, although they may not realize it at the time. If it were possible, and you were to see one of your favorite movies without its background music, you would soon discover the inspiration and feeling is no longer present. Film makers know this: that's why they use background music! Few can honestly say they do not appreciate classical music. They just don't know it yet. If they didn't appreciate background music, and it agitated them, they could not enjoy most movies and television programs. The secret is to put proper music to the story being told, that will capture our interest and motivate us to continue watching.

One of the best examples of what I am trying to say is found in the music of John Williams: for the motion pictures Jurassic Park 1 and 2. Now here is something worth thinking about. Take away the action and the spoken word of these movies, and you are left with what anyone would have to admit—"Now this is beautiful music!" It has harmony, tempo, and meaning and inspiration. This music makes me feel so good: and we need that! The same is true of worship in a church. **We need to set the right inspirational mood to turn one's thoughts toward God, and away from the sounds and sights of the world beyond the church doors.**

Without music, life's story would be very dull. The trouble in these times is that we are being brainwashed to the point of liking the kind of music to which we are exposed on a daily basis, and this is anything but inspirational. One might go so far as to suggest that a person can become tone-deaf to real music, if one is never exposed to it. So . . . as your life story (the story of your life) begins to develop, true music (See definition of music, page 126ff), can become an inspiration toward a more meaningful and fulfilling life. Keep an eye on the truth found in: **Proverbs 22:6 *"To Train up a child in the way he should go; and when he is old, he will not depart from it."***

It is reasonable to assume that persons can learn to enjoy good music from youth on up. Someone has said, "A person must eat 7 olives before one can acquire a taste for them." This may or may not be true. But, how can a person learn to enjoy and experience *better (great) music* if he or she is never exposed to it, or if a person doesn't even want to know what better music is? It is so sad that many individuals never get beyond the **status quo.** Many persons never make an attempt to reach for that which is on a higher plain in the area of music, or in other facets for their lives as well.

The music or sounds of the big bands were not always pleasant to the ear, but at least the instruments were blended together to result in harmonious tones and rhythms. To use *'The Three Little Fishies'* as an example of bad and silly music from the past, in no way settles the argument by asking "And you are critical of today's music?"

Some of the finest big band music was actually taken from a source not known by many today . . . that is the operas, symphonies, and sacred music.

Glenn Miller is considered to be the best big band of all time. His very popular *'Moonlight Sonata,'* was taken from Beethoven's 'Moonlight Sonata.'

The big band of Larry Clinton was one of the first to take melodies from the great symphonies and operas: songs like *'My Reverie,'* from the music of Claude Debussy; and *'Martha,'* from the opera written by Fredrick Von Flotow; and *'I dreamt I dwelt in Marble Halls,'* from the opera by Michael Balfe.

Also, there is Rachmaninoff's Concerto, from which Freddie Martin came up with another very popular song of the day *'Full Moon and Empty Arms.'*

And what about *'Here Comes the Bride,'* which is taken from Lohengrin, an opera written by Richard Wagner. I can remember my mother used too play *'Love's Old Sweet Song,'* on the old upright piano in our home. I doubt she ever realized she was playing music from Richard Wagner's opera, Tannhauser.

Remember 'The Lone Ranger' program? Most viewers do not know that the musical score is taken from *'The William Tell Overture,'* by Gioachino Rossini. The main background core of music for this program was taken from Franz List's *'Les Les Préludes.'* Also, when the horses are on the run (chase) the music of Wagner's opera *'Rienzi'* is used for the background.

Even in the Looney Tune cartoons, the music of Wagner's *'Ride of Die Walkure'* is heard along with other Wagnerian hints.

And then of course there is Beethoven's 9th symphony. Those who are familiar with the great hymns of the church will remember, *'Joyful Joyful, We Adore Thee,'* which was taken from Beethoven's 9th symphony.

The popular song *'Till the End of Time,'* was taken from Chopin's Polonaise.

Also, *'I'm Always Chasing Rainbows,'* is a popular song, but it was originally written by Fredrick Chopin, from his Fantaisie-Impromptu.

And we may also mention Antonin Dvorak's New World Symphony from which the modern well known Negro spiritual *'Goin' Home,'* was taken.

The popular song *'Tonight We Love,'* was made popular by the Freddy Martin's orchestra, and was taken from Tchaikovsky's Piano Concerto in B Flat Minor.

The popular *'Our Love,'* a big band favorite, was taken from Tchaikovsky's Romeo and Juliet.

In Tchaikovsky's 5th symphony, we find the tune, made popular by Glenn Miller and Harry James, that we have come to know as *'Moon Love.'*

Then we have Borodine's 'Polovtsian Dances,' taken from Prince Igor, from which the popular *'Stranger in Paradise,'* was taken.

The prelude to Wagner's opera Parsifal, contains a passage of music which Christian Churches have used for years, and still use as a response to follow prayer, or sometimes at the end of worship: *'The Three Fold Amen.'*

Even our hymnals make use of great contemporary music. The hymn we have recently come to enjoy is *'Lord of the Dance.'* It was written in 1963. At first thought, some considered this to be about dancing. However, this great hymn is speaking of the ministry of Jesus, but the tune comes from Aaron Copland's 'Appalachian Spring.'

Another example: *'God Be with You till We Meet Again,'* is found in the United Methodist Hymnal, but the tune was written by composer:

Ralph Vaughan Williams. There are endless examples of from where great music originated.

When in seminary one of our professors told us that it would be totally out of place to set our great hymns of the Church to the swing sounds of the big bands of that day. Thankfully, I know only a few examples of where the great hymns of the church were set to the sounds of the Big Band. Fortunately, this did not become the norm! Such treatment of the great hymns did not inspire, nor was it lasting.

It is interesting to hear what some musicians can do with the music we have come to know and love. Some time ago, while attending a concert featuring the United States Navy Jazz band 'The Commodores,' the concert ended with one of John Philip Sousa's marches, *'Stars and Stripes Forever.'* I overheard two individuals objecting because it was played to a jazz beat, complaining "This was supposed to be a March!"

Could the Lord be saddened after hearing what we have done with music for worship? While serving a church in California, our pianist played Ave Maria to a swing beat. Our love of Ralph Bowden would not allow any in the congregation to laugh at that moment: we really were tempted. There were a few smiles.

WE ARE AS SHEEP GONE ASTRAY

In this section, we need to take an honest, careful, and unbiased look at Man's confused condition and his background, and then honestly admit the words of **Isaiah 53:6 are true.** *"All we like sheep have gone astray; we have turned every one to his own way; and the LORD hath laid on Jesus the iniquity of us all."* Until a person recognizes the truth of these words, (we like sheep have gone astray) the individual will never *let go and let God* work in his or her life! **This is basic!**

God wants us to be united, yet we compromise the faith when we are constantly trying to please others, so they will like us, and want to come join us. "United we stand, or divided we fall" is not just a great quotation from Benjamin Franklin, but from the lips of many other leaders as well. Confusion results when we compromise the great truths of God's Word.

The looming question today is: *how and when should we worship God?* We just can't seem to make up our minds. Shall we ignore The Lord's Day, so we can have Sunday to do whatever else it may be we have in mind? Shall our services be designed to be attractive to youth (this is a fallacy), at the expense of everyone else in the congregation? And yes . . . what time is best for Worship and Sunday School? Our personal schedules stand before us as road blocks! satan, the father of lies, is the author of confusion. This has divided more congregations than we can list. People can always find a good reason, to look for another church that suits them better. People are often looking for something to criticize, so they will not feel quite so guilty about leaving their church. And to ease their conscience, they never hesitate to tell others what they dislike about their present church.

Even Jesus lost a large part of His audience in **John, chapter 6**. This is the chapter where Jesus feeds the five thousand, after which the disciples boarded their boat to sail across the Sea of Galilee. Soon, they found themselves in troubled waters: literally. Next, they saw Jesus walking on the water. This promoted Peter to step over the edge of the boat, so he could walk on the water to meet Jesus. Peter's fears, in the midst of troubled waters, resulted in Jesus having to save his life. Meanwhile, the great mass of people were following Jesus around the lake to Capernaum. He knew they were following Him for all the wrong reasons. It was when Jesus was talking about Holy Communion, that they thought He was speaking about cannibalism (eating His body and drinking His blood).

John's Gospel 6:48-67 *I am the bread of life.* **49** *Your forefathers ate the manna in the desert, yet they died.* **50** *But here is the bread that comes down from heaven, which a man may eat and not die.* **51** *I am the living bread that came down from heaven. If anyone eats of this bread, he will live forever. This bread is my flesh, which I* *will give for the life of the world."* **52** *Then the Jews began to argue sharply among themselves, "How can this man give us his flesh to eat?"* **53** Jesus said to them, *"I tell you the truth, unless you eat the flesh of the Son of Man and drink his blood, you have no life in you.* **54** *Whoever eats my flesh and drinks my blood has eternal life, and I will raise him up at the last day.* **55** *For my flesh is real food and my blood is real drink.* **56** *Whoever eats my flesh and drinks my blood remains in me, and I in him.* **57** *Just as the living Father sent me and I live because of the Father, so the one who feeds on me will live because of me. this, said, This is an hard saying; who can hear it?* **58** *This is that bread which came down from heaven: not as your fathers did eat manna, and are dead: he that eateth of this bread shall live for ever.* **59** *These things said he in the synagogue, as he taught in Capernaum.* **60** <u>*Many therefore of his disciples, when they had heard this, said, This is an hard saying; who can hear it?*</u> **61** *When Jesus knew in himself that his disciples murmured at it,* he *said* unto *them, Doth this offend you?* **62** *What and if ye shall see the Son of man ascend up where he was before?* **63** *It is the spirit that quickeneth; the flesh profiteth nothing: the words that I speak unto you, they are spirit, and they are life.* **64** *But there are some of you that believe not. For Jesus knew from* the *beginning who* they *were* that *believed not, and who should betray him.* **65** *And* he *said, Therefore said I unto you, that no man can come unto me, except it were given unto him of my Father.* **66** *From that* time *many of his disciples went back, and walked* no *more with him.* **67** <u>*Then said Jesus* unto the *twelve, Will ye also go away?*</u>

By the Grace of God the disciples did not walk away from Jesus to go their own way, as others did when they refused to accept truth!

CHURCH SHOPPING—HOPPING

We all know people who go from one church to another. They will drive miles to hear some evangelist speak . . . but they cannot find a local church that will satisfy them. If they are looking for the *perfect church*, they will never find it, for once they join that *perfect church*, it suddenly becomes imperfect! Need we ask why? Ask these individuals if they would consider the original 12 Apostles to be the *perfect church*. No doubt they would be caught off guard enough to say "Yes." This would be a good time to remind them that Judas betrayed the Lord, Thomas doubted the Lord, and Peter even denied knowing Jesus three times, and was always speaking before he thought. We have these same imperfections in our lives as well.

It could be said, "Perhaps it doesn't matter what church you stay away from, if you can't have things your way!" One cannot be a Christian and stay away from corporate worship, and the fellowship that goes with it: unless that person is incapacitated in some manner, or is ill on a given Sunday. One will very seldom miss corporate worship, if they are really walking with Christ.

Have you ever gone up to a new comer in your church to greet and hopefully get a positive response, only to hear "Oh, we are church shopping." **Dr. Ken Carter,** senior pastor of Providence United Methodist Church in Charlotte, N.C. reminds us of how *church shopping* reminds him of the children's story of the Three Bears. One soup was too hot, another to cold, but finally one was just right. The fact is we are quite like this children's story when it comes to *church shopping.* We make these decisions in all areas of our lives. It is quite a sad commentary on those of us who seek to worship God, that we get caught up in **worship wars**.

Today the church is being disgraced, and divided by the *various ideas* being brought into the church, as to how one should worship. We all have our favorite ways to worship, and the type of music is often made the main target. If the music touches one's heart, that is inspiration—that is one thing, but if the music makes you want to dance and sway around . . . or whatever—that is entertainment. Can a praise team with singer/s guitar/s, keyboard, drums, etc., take place of the pipe organ or pianist? Worshipers may be praising the performers: not the Lord. If you don't think so, then listen to the conversation following worship. "I sure liked that keyboard artist, or those singers, and the guitar was played very well." We really like to be entertained, and experience that feel good part of worship. However, this is not what we are about when it comes to Biblical Worship. We do need to come to grips with what we are doing, because we say we are praising the Lord. Souls are being lost while we play around being "tossed to and fro by every wind and doctrine." **Ephesians 4:14-15.** *"That we henceforth be no more children, tossed to and fro, and carried about with every wind of doctrine, by the sleight of men, and cunning craftiness, whereby they lie in wait to deceive."* **15** *But speaking the truth in love, may grow up into him in all things, which is the head, even Christ:"*

In one of the churches I served, the term *'praise music'* was introduced to the congregation by two well meaning individuals. In the bulletin these tunes were identified *as "praise music".* The title and words of this *'praise music'* were printed on paper from which we were to sing, accompanied by a CD on a boom box (a radio/CD combination). The implication was that the great hymns we had been singing were not praise music. The inconvenience of trying to sing to printed words on sheets of paper, eventually led to a large screen and projector, so the congregation could more easily see the words they were to sing. Eventually, this led to a praise band. The church now has two services, one traditional and one contemporary. The congregation is now a divided, all brought about by one or two persons, because of personal music preferences. This has now led to two churches meeting in the same building. Time schedules are difficult to arrange, for the pastor and congregation. Friends do not see many of their friends at worship anymore.

Worship is not a program designed for entertainment. There is a huge difference between being inspired which leads to motivation for service, and entertainment to give one a temporary high.

We all need to be keenly aware of the fact that worship is influenced and shaped by the very content within the service. "For if we don't have doctrinal stability, we cannot have ethical stability, and if we don't have ethical stability we don't have stability of worship, and if we don't have stability of worship, we are no longer related vitally and necessarily to the headship of Jesus Christ. Our historic boundaries would become lost in a post-modern sea of autonomous self-definitions." (Dr. Timothy Tennent, President of Asbury Theological seminary in Wilmore Kentucky).

Worship should guide us through the process of redemption and response to God. The best guide for a Christian is the deep and living tradition of the Old and New Testaments, filled with guidance about worship. In Scripture we read about Passover feasts, an Upper Room, extended sermons, intercessory prayers, songs of praise, and psalms of lamentation, baptisms and offerings, benedictions, and processionals toward and recessionals from the throne of God.

Doing things the way we have always done, does not mean we are worshiping in a way that pleases God. The traditional worship services, along with the contemporary services of today are not all they should be! What is your answer to the question of how we should worship Almighty God? Well, your answer doesn't really matter because you get a different answer from every individual you ask. This is part of our problem: we all want worship to be done *our way*.

Jesus told us that He is **the way**, the **truth** and the **life**. Jesus does not give us an outline for corporate worship. He did give His disciples an outline for how to pray, and therefore we have *The Lord's Prayer*. Jesus also said: "No one can come to the Father except by Me." If you want to approach the Father God, it must be done through Jesus. Is it possible to know God without going through Jesus? We will look at Job next for the answer to this question. Job's experiences took place before Jesus was sent of God. Jesus was and is the reflection of the Father. Jesus did give us the Beatitudes, which lay out for us the way we ought to be thinking. I like to break the word beatitude down so it looks like be-attitude.

The beatitudes: **Matthew 5:1-12** *"And seeing the multitudes, he (Jesus) went up into a mountain: and when he was set, his disciples came unto him: 2 And he opened his mouth, and taught them, saying, 3 Blessed are the poor in spirit: for theirs is the kingdom of heaven. 4 Blessed are they that mourn: for they shall be comforted. 5 Blessed are the meek: for they shall inherit the earth. 6 Blessed are they which do hunger and thirst after righteousness: for they shall be filled. 7 Blessed are the merciful: for they shall obtain mercy. 8 Blessed are the pure in heart: for they shall see God. 9 Blessed are the peacemakers: for they shall be called the children of God. 10 Blessed are they which are persecuted for righteousness' sake: for theirs is the kingdom of heaven. 11 Blessed are ye, when men shall revile you, and persecute you, and shall say all manner of evil against you falsely, for my sake. 12 Rejoice, and be exceeding glad: for great is your reward in heaven: for so persecuted they the prophets which were before you.* KJV

We need an attitude adjustment!

Next (below) we shall take a good look at Job to see how he thought of God. We should think of God as Job thought of Him. We can't worship God, if we really don't know Him. Our knowledge of God is reflected in the music we hear and sing while at worship. Much of today's contemporary music is so repetitive, and shallow both in content, and in musicality (acceptable rhythm and harmony). God knows what we are up to at any given split second. He knows all of us through and through! The Apostle Paul knew his condition as a sinner. In **Romans 7:24** the Apostle Paul makes his confession: *"What a wretched man I am! Who will rescue me from this body of death?"* NIV

We need to humble ourselves, within the reality of who we are: human beings created in God's image, but fallen creatures: therefore sinners! God knows all about this, therefore He sent His Son to die for our sins.

DID JOB KNOW GOD?

In the book of **Job 1:1** *"There was a man from the land of Uz whose name was Job; and that man was <u>blameless and upright</u>, and one who feared God and shunned evil."*

Let us take an honest look at Job and see how he felt when he faced serious, overwhelming problems in his life. Job's friends felt they had the solution to all his problems. Job's friends told him, **"Job you are a sinner."** However, we know that Job was blameless and upright and feared God and shunned evil. He was very wealthy: he had 7 sons, 3 daughters, 7,000 sheep, 3,000 camels, 500 yoke of oxen, 500 donkeys and many servants. This is really telling us that: no matter how rich you are in this world today, you could not out do Job's wealth in the world of his day. He was simply as wealthy or rich as any man could be on this planet at that time! satan thought he had the answer to Job's wealth. His motives for serving God faithfully paid off . . . he had a good thing going with God. **Job 1:8** *"Does Job fear God for nothing?"* satan was sure that if God would no longer bless him, he would end up cursing God. *So the trial begins.* First, God gave satan permission to strip Job of all his wealth, but satan was told he could not harm Job physically. satan still refuses to give up. Next, God gave satan permission to attack Job's flesh, but not to take his life. Then Job's wife to advises him to curse God and die. **(Job 2:9)** Thus far Job, as a man of God, has given two responses to satan's attacks: with which we are so blessed to know: **[1] Job 1:21** *"Naked came I into this world (my mother's womb), and, and naked shall I return to the Lord."* **[2]** *"Shall we receive good at the hand of God, and not receive bad."* In all of this Job did not sin against the Lord God. <u>**Job knew God**</u>! **Job 19:26** *"And though after my skin worms destroy this body, yet in my flesh I* **shall** *see God."*

Have you ever found yourself asking the question, "<u>Why me God?</u>" Many of us have found ourselves with this same question on our mind: several times. We desperately try to make sense of a seemingly hopeless situation. We look for *holes*: and fill them with oft used meaningless clichés that are really of little help. Know that God never fails us, but we do fail Him.

JOBS THREE FRIENDS

Job has three friends: their names are—Eliphaz, Bildad, and Zophar. We have friends like Job's in our churches and communities today, however their names are much more palatable. How do we deal with well meaning friends? How did Job handle his friends? Remember these friends of job were *most sincere*. They even had a meeting to see how they could be of help to Job. They wanted to comfort Job. **Job 2:11** *"Now when Job's three friends heard of all this evil that was come upon him, they came every one from his own place: Eliphaz the Temanite, and Bildad the Shuhite, and Zophar the Naamathite: for they had made an appointment together to come to mourn with him and to comfort him."*

The suffering of Job was so great these 3 friends were dumfounded. Seven days and nights passed before they could say a word to Job. Before they could say anything, Job began the dialogue by cursing the day he was born. So now here is the advice from these 3 friends of Job.

Eliphaz told Job: *"Job you are suffering because you are a sinner. Go to God and confess your sins to God."*

Bildad asks Job *"How long will you keep blowing words around like wind? If you were not a sinner God would hear your prayers and bless your home. Remember Job, God will not cast away a good man nor prosper evildoers. So you are not a good man."*

Zophar speaks next: *"When you mock God, shouldn't someone make you feel ashamed? You claim you are pure in the eyes of God. I wish God would speak and tell you what he thinks of you Job. I wish you could see yourself Job, as God sees you: for God knows everything you have done. Listen to me Job: God is doubtless punishing you far* *less than you deserve. Before you turn to God and stretch out you hands to him, get rid of your sins and leave all iniquity behind you."*

JOB'S CONCEPT OF GOD

These three friends of Job had their minds made up: Job was a sinner, and this is why he was being tried. No amount of logic would help. <u>The bottom line is this:</u> **<u>these three friends of Job did not know the God they were professing!</u>** *They were brimming with sincerely, but lacked Godly humility.* The fact is they didn't really know God or Job. They were to eager to pass judgment. They could not really find a way to help Job. *Job agrees* that he is the sinner they claim him to be.

Now, Job is concerned as to how he can be exonerated before God. What Job doesn't know is that God has already weighed in on his situation. Job realizes that his only hope was to get an audience with God. God already knows what is going on, but Job hasn't found out yet. God lives in eternity, while Job and all of us are living by the clock and calendar. Yet, in those early days (relatively speaking) Job had a profound understanding of Who God is. This is one of the great passages for **praise and worship**. For here Job outlines the attributes of God like you will find nowhere else. Job is saying ***"Let me tell you Who this God is!"*** Job gives us **<u>6 powerful statements about the nature of God</u>**: "The Grace-Filled Life" **by Maxie Dunnam** (Used by permission)

(1) God is **Incomprehensible**. **(2)** God is **Invincible**. He is mighty in strength beyond our ability to comprehend. **(3)** God is **Invulnerable.** You cannot harden yourself against God and win the battle. He is stronger than any person or weapon we can conceive or dream of on earth. **(4)** God is **Incredible.** He does great things past our finding out. He removes the mountains. He shakes the earth out of its place. He commands the sun and it does not rise. He seals off the stars, and walks on the waves of the sea. He commands the heavens. He does great things past finding out. Job asks, "Do you know what God is like? He is incredible. Everything you see God has created!" Job asks his friends (Eliphaz, Bildad and Zophar) "Do you see the God with Whom I have to deal?" **(5)** God is **Invisible**. If He goes by me, I can't see Him. Who has ever looked upon the face of God and lived? This brings to mind **Exodus 33:20** where it reads: *And God said to Moses: "Thou canst not see my face: for there shall no man see me and live."* KJV **(6)** God is **Irresistible**. If He gives and He takes away, who can hinder Him. We cannot stop the plans of God, even if we don't understand them, nor want them to happen. Who can say to God, "What are You doing?" So Job has this *awesome* concept of Who God is. A summation—God is: **Incomprehensible, Invincible, Invulnerable, Incredible, Invisible, and Irresistible!**

I wish everyone (including myself) could have this holy, realistic concept of God as Job exhibited! *Job had this incredible respect for God* and this kept him humble, and in his place as a child of God. How can someone so small (as Job, or as you and I) ever connect with a God? This was Job's problem, and it is our problem as well. We hope the way we worship will help make this vital connection with God, but often we are our own worst enemies! We come to worship with a similar mind set as was seen in Job's three friends . . . Eliphaz, Bildad, and Zophar.

So now we come to the heart of the matter: Job speaks volumes of wisdom concerning the God revealed in the Holy Bible, and the source of salvation. In essence, Job lists some very pertinent statements and questions (See Job 9):

1. How can a mortal be just before God?
2. If God decides to argue with a human, can a person answer even one question out of a thousand He may ask?
3. God is so wise and mighty, therefore, has anyone ever opposed Him successfully?
4. God moves mountains, overturning them in His anger.
5. God shakes the earth to its foundations.

6. The sun won't rise; the stars won't shine if He commands it so.

7. God alone has stretched out the heaven and trampled the waves of the sea.

8. God alone made the Bear (Big Dipper), Orion and the Pleiades and the constellations of the southern Zodiac.

9. God does incredible miracles: too many to count.

10. He passes by me and I do not see Him. He moves on and I do not perceive Him.

11. When God sends death to take an individual away, who can stop Him?

12. Who dares ask of God, "What are you doing?"

13. Who am I that I should argue with Almighty God or even reason with Him?

14. Though I am innocent, I cannot answer Him: I must appeal for mercy to my accuser. If I prayed to God and my prayers were answered I would barely believe that God heard my cry.

15. For God crushes me with a tempest, and multiplies my wounds without cause, and even though He will not let me get my breath, but fills me with bitterness: if this were a contest of strength, He is the strong one! God alone is strong and just. Who can argue with Him?

16. I am blameless; I do not know myself. I loath my life.

17. God destroys both the blameless and the wicked.

18. When disaster brings sudden death, He mocks at the calamity of the innocent.

19. The earth is given into the hand of the wicked; he covers the eyes of its judges: if it is not He, who then its it?

20. My days are swifter than a runner; they flee away, they see no good.

21. God is not a mortal, as I am, that I might answer Him.

22. There is no mediator between us who might lay his hand on us both.

23. Who can stand before the authority of God?
24. I will speak without fear of God, for I know I am not what I am thought to be.

Do we see ourselves in any of the above 24 statements? Job was not going to betray or curse the all powerful (Omnipotent) God, for he is being wrongfully accused, misjudged and totally misunderstood by his friends! Have you ever felt like Job?

When all is said and done, to make it simple for all who read this: God asks very little of us, except that we *"do justly, love mercy and walk humbly before Him."* **Micah 6:8** NIV

After carefully considering Job's responses, it appears that *Job did know God*, and knew Him much better than we who are living in the enlighten age of the New Testament teachings. Job didn't have all the answers and we certainly do not have all the answers about Jehovah God! So—we must live by faith!

Wow! **God is Holy**! Any other terms we use to describe God, from our human understanding, fall short of what or who God is! You can deny Him, but that does not change Him. You can ignore God, but that does not change Him. You can be disrespectful toward God, but that does not change Him. You can disagree with God, and that doesn't change Him. You can deny God, but if you do, you better get your act together before you have committed the unpardonable sin (blaspheme against the Holy Spirit). **The Holy Spirit is constantly and tirelessly seeking to get our attention, that He may convict us of sin, with the glorious response that we repent and accept God's plan of salvation through the Lamb of God, Who takes away the sins of the world!** It is as simple as that! If you reject God's plan for salvation, you are committing the unforgivable sin, and hopefully you will not die in that state! But know this . . . ignoring the Scripture, and being outside the fellowship of the saints, and turning a deaf ear to the Holy Spirit, along with the presence of Christ at Holy Communion by faith—you are on your own—and living dangerously! Job knew he was a sinner, but he also knew that he feared God and stayed away from evil (sin). He was most blessed for being the kind of faith-filled man he was: not stubborn: but standing on solid ground, knowing that God had <u>brought him this far</u> . . . (this is the basic meaning of the word **Ebenezer)** in the great hymn *'Come Thou Font of Every Blessing.'* Not being on the same page as her husband, Job's wife told him to curse God and die.

Now we come to Jobs three major and important reservations about God that help us understand the frustrations Job was feeling. These same frustrations are felt by us in today's world. **(1)** Job couldn't *dispute* with God. God is omniscient (knows all), omnipresent (everywhere present), and omnipotent (all powerful), and if he (Job) were ever to make contact with God, he wouldn't believe it was Him. We also can say along with Job: Who am I that God would ever listen to me?

Look at the experience Samuel had when staying with Eli: **I Samuel 3:4-10,** *"Then the LORD called Samuel. Samuel answered, "Here I am." 5 And he ran to Eli and said, "Here I am; you called me." But Eli said, "I did not call; go back and lie down." So he went and lay down. 6 Again the LORD called, "Samuel!" And Samuel got up and went to Eli and said, "Here I am; you called me." "My son," Eli said, "I did not call; go back and lie down." 7 Now Samuel did not yet know the LORD: The word of the LORD had not yet been revealed to him. 8 The LORD called Samuel a third time, and Samuel got up and went to Eli and said, "Here I am; you called me." Then Eli realized that the LORD was calling the boy. 9 So Eli told Samuel, "Go and lie down, and if he calls you, say, 'Speak, LORD, for your servant is listening.' "So Samuel went and lay down in his place. 10 The LORD came and stood there, calling as at the other times, "Samuel! Samuel!"Then Samuel said, "<u>Speak, for your servant is listening</u>."* NIV

Samuel couldn't believe God was calling him. God calls us, and wants a relationship with us: **on His terms!** Job couldn't *Make* a **Deal** with God. We certainly cannot make deals with God. Job says: "If I were to call God and He answered me, I wouldn't even believe it was His voice." **(2)** Job couldn't even *Direct* God; that is to tell God what

He should or should not do. God is strong and final, and Job didn't stand a chance against God. Job felt that if he could make connections with God, who is going to set it up anyway? God is strong and just. Who is going to defend Job if he were to go to court? **(3)** We notice that Job says he couldn't even *depend* on God. (Maxie Dunnam inspired (Used by permission)

Job 9:20-25 *Even if I were innocent, my mouth would condemn me; if I were blameless, it would pronounce me guilty. 21 "Although I am blameless, I have no concern for myself; I despise my own life. 22 It is all the same; that is why I say, 'He destroys both the blameless and the wicked.' 23 When a scourge brings sudden death, he mocks the despair of the innocent. 24 When a land falls into the hands of the wicked, he blindfolds its judges. If it is not he, then who is it? 25 "My days are swifter than a runner; they fly away without a glimpse of joy."* NIV

But now hear this; Job says: "If it is not God, then who is doing all this, to me, then who is?" "What I need is for God to set things straight!"

Job is saying: "My friends do not understand me, therefore they come to the wrong conclusion about me. What they are saying about me is just not true. I think I know what is going on in my own heart, but I am beginning to doubt it. I know I cannot manipulate God to set things straight as they were at one time, when all was going so very well for me and mine." BUT, remember: after all was said and done, God did put Job back to his former prosperity and blessings. Job just had to remain faithful, and patient! He refused to run ahead of God!

Job needed someone to represent him before God, in God's courtroom. We all know who is able to do this. **Revelation 5:12-13** *"Worthy is the Lamb that was slain to receive power, and riches, and wisdom, and strength, and honour, and glory, and blessing. 13 And every creature which is in heaven, and on the earth, and under the earth, and such as are in the sea, and all that are in them, heard I saying, Blessing, and honour, and glory, and power, be unto him that sitteth upon the throne, and unto the Lamb for ever and ever."* KJV

The very Son of God represents You and me before the throne of God! He is the great attorney defending our/my case.

There is no doubt that Job knew God, and that God was in complete control! So far as we are concerned, we now have the New Testament teachings to help us come to know that Jesus is our friend! However, God is God, and we cannot tell Him what He is like, any more than Job could.

OUR CONCEPT OF GOD

We have all heard the phrase "Don't get the cart before the horse." In other words, don't get things backwards or out of order. We need to be careful to get our **theology** (Knowledge of God) **correct** and **straight**! Many times we speak of God as "Our God, or My God." We go so far as to sing, "Our God is an Awesome God." The fact is we belong to God . . . we are His . . . children, created in His image, and this is what is awesome. He does not belong to us! The expressions we use when speaking of God, come from at least one or more of three sources. **(1)** Our concept of God evolves from what we have heard others say about God . . . (hearsay), or **(2)** We formulate our thoughts of God as we experience His blessings in day by day living, and **(3)** Our concept and knowledge of God is taken from the Word of God as revealed in Scripture.

The words to the song, "Our God is an Awesome God," imply that we have chosen God from the bank of other Gods of the world; and, have come to the conclusion that our God is better than all the other Gods we have studied. But, the fact is—there are no other God's! Oh yes . . . there are many gods. But know this; The God Who reveals Himself to us does not belong to us! We belong to Him! The word awesome is a humanistic adjective, that doesn't quite cut it when trying to praise God. Your appearance may be awesome, the music is awesome, the weather is awesome, everything is or may be awesome, but God is infinitely more than the word awesome implies! So, let us try to grow in our Biblical understanding and express ourselves on an <u>ever growing level</u>. It is only because of His grace that we can even approach Him. He has revealed Himself to us through Scripture, and through His Son, and **this is indeed what is awesome**! You may think I am 'nitpicking' and perhaps I am to prove a point . . . we are so content *with the status quo and the popular trends*. We thoughtlessly repeat what has become popular, and used with no further consideration or thought.

We know there are other gods, and we have not only made them: we have become one of them. Hear again **Genesis 3:5** The devil is speaking to Eve: ***"For God knows that when you eat of it your eyes will be opened, and you will be <u>like</u> God, knowing good and evil."*** The truth is, we did not become like God, **<u>we became like gods</u>**: we know good *and* evil, <u>but</u> the tragic thing is—we *don't really know good <u>from</u> evil.* **Isaiah 5:20** ***"Woe to those who call evil good and good evil, who put darkness for light and light for darkness, who put bitter for sweet and sweet for bitter."*** NIV

The word *awesome* is not the only word we use when trying to identify and define our feelings toward God.

In today's vernacular everything is *<u>cool</u>*. My comeback to that shallow and much **over used** comment is: "If it's *<u>cool</u>*, that means *<u>it's not so" hot</u>.*" We used to use the word *'<u>hot</u>'* as an expression of agreement; like we also use the word awesome for an experience or event with which we are pleased. We used to say, "Wow man . . . your car is really <u>hot</u>. In fact that is where the phrase *'hot rod'* was born. The English language uses many such expressions, slang or otherwise, that really mean nothing, but are an indication we need to learn how to speak English, and say what we really mean. We need to find appropriate adjectives to describe our feelings. To say this or that is *cool*, or *hot* takes no thought or education. So think about what is being said. Stop doing what everyone else is doing; and, be you own person. God is <u>not cool or hot</u>! We certainly have not earned His blessings; that's why we call it what it is—**Not**—*cool* or *hot* . . . it is **God's *grace***. My hope, at this point, is that God's children learn to show God the respect due Him, daily and at corporate worship! We should stop trying to be popular through the use the endless contemporary words which, as some think, make us *hep* or *with it,* i.e., *real cool.* We need to get back to good and proper English in our speech, and stop trying to be contemporary through the use of words that have only shallow or no real meaning at best! Years ago we quite often would say, with regards to the way things happen: *"That's the way the cookie crumbles."* or *"That's the way the ball bounces."* Some tell us the English language is one of the most difficult to learn because we have so many shallow and confusing expressions used in daily conversation. We need to get back to proper English! Considering all God has done, and is yet doing for us is not awesome . . . it is God's Grace. So . . . memorize **Matthew 5:37** reads *"Simply let your 'Yes' be 'Yes,' and your 'No,' be 'No'; anything beyond this <u>comes from the evil one</u>."* God is Grace-filled! This hymn states it clearly:

God of grace and God of glory,
On Thy people pour Thy power.
Crown Thine ancient church's story,
Bring her bud to glorious flower.
Grant us wisdom, grant us courage,
For the facing of this hour,
For the facing of this hour.

It would be so inspiring if we could be more Christ-like, and stop all our vain attempts to be in tune with the crowd in order to be popular and contemporary. Regardless of our age, race, wealth, education or whatever . . . God is calling individuals through His Holy Spirit . . . and that is called **Grace!** There is nothing else like it—that compares to it—or can ever replace it!!!

There is too much confusion as to how we should worship God! A dear well meaning friend said to me recently: "We shall just have to agree to disagree, as to how we should worship." Have we ever thought about what this statement really means? It sounds so cordial, fair, and just plain friendly. In truth it means . . . "I am not going to give another thought to your considerations about worship. I disagree with you, and I am going to worship the way my friends and I prefer. I am not going to change. I am going to a church that does things the way that pleases me. All my friends agree with the way I think, and I intend to keep it that way."

In other words a <u>deadlock has formed</u> and no further growth or learning is likely to take place! Please give thought to what Amos is saying in **Amos 3:3 *"Can two walk together except they be agreed?"*** KJV

The answer is obvious . . . "No . . . they cannot walk together very far, before divisions, arguments and disagreements come to the surface." This reminds me of the old Scottish tune we have all heard: "You take the high road, and I'll take the low road, and I'll be in Scotland before you." We know that our Salvation doesn't work this way. There is only one road or way. That *Way* is Jesus! Read the entire book of Amos . . . it is speaking about good old common sense! Amos is trying to tell us that we need unity and order in our lives, even in the way we worship the Lord our Creator!

In the movie "Seven days in Utopia" these words of great wisdom are to be found, "*I got a lot of **respect** for **tradition** and a **passion** for truth*." And where do we find truth? It is time to look for **truth as found in Scripture** . . . in fact Jesus calls <u>Himself</u> truth. **John 14:6**.

We look for companionship and fellowship with others who *think* like we think, rather than for *truth*. This is how sects, denominations, lodges, clubs, etc. came into existence. When persons feel the need for fellowship, they seek out others of similar mind and interests. Then, they affiliate with one or more of these groups for fellowship and support. <u>However, when we find others who feel like we do at worship, this does not necessarily mean that we are worshiping God in the unity of one spirit</u>! We are not praising the Lord when we bring our whims (desires and ways) into the church. Could it be **we don't know as much about God as we think?** God doesn't need us to tell Him what He is like, as is so often repeated in much contemporary music. The Bible already tells us what God is like, and what He expects of us.

What we do know is, that we are being led, and molded and shaped, by the *exposures* we are experiencing and are witnessing on a daily basis! We are heavily influenced by that to which we are being exposed, in our homes, when with our friends, what we do for entertainment, what we see on television and in the movies; and, also by that which is going on in our community and world. Hopefully, our greatest exposure is to the *truth* as revealed in The Holy Bible, along with sacred worship at the church of our choice, coupled with Bible study classes in church and at home. Our greatest need is to get back to the Bible: its wisdom and truth. Remember, God is Holy. He is the Creator, and our personal Savior: all of this according to **His** plan!

It is not a stretch of the truth to say that anything we put before God may easily become our god. And here comes very difficult words from the mouth of Jesus, but it is not our choice to deny them: *"Anyone who loves his father or mother more than me is not worthy of me, anyone who loves his son or daughter more than me is not worthy of me."*

Jesus is saying you may love your father and mother: they gave you life, but . . . I am come that you might have **life eternal**. No parent can give you eternal life: neither can any of your family members give you eternal life. It is only Jesus who offers eternal life, therefore, we should love Him more for that reason . . . yes even more than father and mother. We may find it difficult to accept these words of Jesus at this moment in our lives. Like Thomas, we want to see before we will believe. None-the-less, we have no choice when it comes to believing. We have to believe and accept the words of Jesus: yes, if only by faith! Even Jesus had to prove to His disciples, and especially Thomas, that he was not a ghost. He invited Thomas to tough His real risen body. **John 20:27-30** *"Then he said to Thomas, 'Put your finger here; see my hands. Reach out your hand and put it into my side. Stop doubting and believe.'"* **28** *Thomas said to him, "My Lord and my God!"* **29** *Then Jesus told him, "Because you have seen me, you have believed;*

blessed are those who have not seen and yet have believed." 30 Jesus did many other miraculous signs in the presence of his disciples, which are not recorded in this book.

Our concept of God is revealed in the music we sing, especially at corporate worship. Think about the words being sung at all times and in all places! Is it truth? During the Christmas season some radio stations were playing a new seasonal song *'Christmas Was Made for Children.'* This sort of heresy is easy to discern, though it is pleasing to many families with children. How many have really given thought about the truth of this so called Christmas tune? This is heresy of the worst kind! Christmas is for <u>all peoples</u> regardless of their age, because it celebrates the birth of Christ. (**John 3:16**). This is the only truthful way to speak of Christmas. Give thought to the theological (Biblical) content of songs used in worshiping the Lord, during one's Christmas and Easter observances, as well as at all services that honor our Savior!

GOD'S ATTRIBUTES

What term can best describe God? We could say that God is Omnipresent (everywhere present), Omniscient (all knowing), and Omnipotent (all powerful) and He is! However, it would be difficult to set any of those words to music. Holy, on the other hand, refers to that which is *set apart*. There would be nothing if it weren't for God. The best adjective we can possibly use when referring to God is '<u>Holy</u>!' There is no reality so *set apart . . . so Holy is* as God! He is much more than awesome! However, if you must cling to the adjective *awesome* when speaking of God, then know this . . . the only thing that really matters is: Have you accepted Jesus Christ as your personal Lord and Savior. Praise God Who desires to save and forgive! We pray "Our Father Who art in heaven . . . <u>hallowed</u> be Thy Name." Hallowed refers to that which is Holy. One of our favorite hymns we enjoy singing; and that best *praises*, and *describes* God, is "Holy, Holy, Holy!" Here the word *Holy* has already been used as an adjective to describe and praise God. We all know and have sung this hymn.

1. Holy, holy, holy! Lord God Almighty!
Early in the morning our song shall rise to thee.
Holy, holy, holy! Merciful and mighty,
God in three persons, blessed Trinity!
2. Holy, holy, holy! All the saints adore thee, casting down their golden crowns around the glassy sea; cherubim and seraphim falling down before thee, which wert, and art, and evermore salt be.
3. Holy, holy, holy! Though the darkness hide thee, though the eye of sinful man thy glory may not see, only thou art holy; there is none beside thee, perfect in power, in love and purity.
4. Holy, holy, holy! Lord God Almighty!
All thy works shall praise thy name, in earth and sky and sea.
Holy, holy, holy! Merciful and mighty,
God in three persons, blessed Trinity.

Below are some Scriptures that may help us understand. We definitely need to lift our stance and seek higher ground when we worship and praise God as Holy. God is not only Holy: He is the only God!

Isaiah 5:15 *"But the LORD of hosts shall be exalted in judgment, and God that is holy shall be sanctified in righteousness." NIV*

Psalm 99:9 *"Exalt the LORD our God, and worship at his holy hill; for the LORD our God is holy." NIV*

Psalm 99:5 *"Exalt ye the LORD our God, and worship at his footstool; for he is holy."* KJV

1 Samuel 6:20 *"And the men of Bethshemesh said, Who is able to stand before this holy LORD God? and to whom shall he go up from us?"*
KJV

Isaiah 45:22 *"Turn to me and be saved, all you ends of the earth; for I am God, and there is no other." NIV*

Isaiah 46:9 *"Remember the former things, those of long ago; I am God, and there is no other; I am God, and there is none like me."* NIV

Joel 2:27 *"Then you will know that I am in Israel, that I am the LORD your God, and that there is no other; never again will my people be shamed."* NIV

Mark 12:32 *"Well said, teacher," the man replied. "You are right in saying that God is one and there is no other but him."* NIV

We are incurably religious, so we will either have God or gods in our life. We need to think this through very carefully and prayerfully, since much of the contemporary expressions used today, give the idea that we know all about God. God is revealed in and through His Son.

John 1:18 *"No man hath* seen *God at any time; the only begotton Son, which is in the bosom of the Father, he hath declared him."* KJV

PLAYING FAVORITES?

God will never let us down, even if it appears that He has! Try to remember, at the same time, He is not to be treated as one may treat a best friend. If we treat God like we treat our friends, we are in trouble! When we look at Jesus, realistically, we are looking at the Son of God, and not the Father. (See **John 14:9** below) Remember the relationship Jesus had with his Father . . . not only was Jesus about His Father's business, He also prayed to His Father. Yet if you want to see what the Father is like, then look to Jesus. We sometimes forget that Jesus HUMBLED HIMSELF, for the time He was on earth; when the Father sent Him as recorded in **John 3:16**, a passage of Scripture we know by heart. **John 14:9** *"Jesus saith unto him, Have I been so long time with you, and yet hast thou not known me Philip? He that hath seen me hath seen the Father."* KJV Again in The Good News Translation: *"Jesus answered, "For a long time I have been with you all; yet you do not know me, Philip? Whoever has seen me has seen the Father.*

Why, then, do you say, 'Show us the Father'?" God was on the mission of saving us from our sin, when <u>he Sent His Son</u> to earth.

We do not know Jesus, if we think of Him as a special friend holding hands with us, as we stroll sentimentally down road of life. Jesus does not play favorites. He is with us, but not to grant us special favors. In **John 16:12** we read: *And in that day ye shall ask me nothing. Verily, verily, I say unto you, Whatsoever ye shall <u>ask the Father</u> in my name, he will give it to you.* KJV

It would be nice if we could have such a buddy buddy relationship with Jesus, so we would ask special favors from Him at any time! He is much more than this sort of friend; so let us not loose sight of this fact. Many try to make bargains with God such as: "If you heal me, or let my loved one live, (and the endless list goes on) then I will be a better person." Look at what two of the disciples (James and John) wanted out of their relationship with Jesus. They tried to use that friendship with Jesus, to their own benefit.

Mark 10:35-41 *"Then James and John, the sons of Zebedee, came to him. "Teacher," they said, "we want you to do for us whatever we ask." 36 "What do you want me to do for you?" he asked. 37 They replied, "Let one of us sit at your right and the other at your left in your glory." 38 "You don't know what you are asking," Jesus said. "Can you drink the cup I drink or be baptized with the baptism I am baptized with?" 39 "We can," they answered. Jesus said to them, "You will drink the cup I drink and be baptized with the baptism I am baptized with, 40 but to sit at my right or left is not for me to grant. These places belong to those for whom they have been prepared." 41 When the ten heard about this, they became indignant with James and John."* NIV

Yes, Jesus is our Savior/Friend, yet His words are sometimes as hard as nails; and, truth hurts like a driven nail! In Matthew 10:**36**-42 *"A man's enemies will be the members of his own household.' 37 "Anyone who loves his father or mother more than me is not worthy of me; anyone who loves his son or daughter more than me is not* *worthy of me; 38 and anyone who does not take his cross and follow me is not worthy of me. 39 Whoever finds his life will lose it, and whoever loses his life for my sake will find it. 40 "He who receives you receives me, and he who receives me receives the one who sent me. 41 Anyone who receives a prophet because he is a prophet will receive a prophet's reward, and anyone who receives a righteous man because he is a righteous man will receive a righteous man's reward. 42 And if anyone gives even a cup of cold water to one of these little ones because he is my disciple, I tell you the truth, he will certainly not lose his reward."* NIV

We sing *"What a Friend We Have in Jesus"* and this is certainly true; but He is a friend in a very special way that goes far beyond what our friends on this earth can offer. This is true because Jesus is <u>our only hope</u> . . . our personal Savior. **John 3:16** *"For God so loved the world that he <u>gave</u> his one and only Son, that whoever believes in him shall not perish but have eternal life."* **NIV In Proverbs 18:24 we read** *"A man that hath friends must shew himself friendly: and there is a friend that sticketh closer than a brother."* KJV

The following passage speaks of how Isaiah spoke of God: **Isaiah 9:6** *"For unto us a child is born, unto us a Son is given; and the government shall be upon His shoulder; and His name shall be called <u>Wonderful</u>, <u>Counselor</u>, <u>The Mighty God</u>, <u>the Everlasting Father</u>, <u>The Prince of Peace</u>."* KJV

A professor in seminary compared these words to the ringing out of a bell, as the clapper strikes the edge of the bell from side to side with each tug of the bell ringer: "Wonderful" . . . "Counselor" . . . "The Mighty God" . . . "The Everlasting Father" . . . "The Prince of Peace." Let this ring in your mind. Isaiah is talking about praise phrases that refer to Jesus!

So treat Jesus with all the dignity, reverence, humility, thoughtfulness, love, kindness, and honesty that is due Him: as you would do unto God! God knows when we are acting contrary to His will. This means, as we walk with our Savior, there should be no more filthy talk, cursing or blasphemous thoughts! There can be no more sentimental *good feeling* **ego trips**, as though one were closer to God than others, or even deserved, a special place in the heart of God. This also means *no more judging* of one another.

Romans 5:6-8 *"You see, at just the right time, when we were still powerless, Christ died for the ungodly. 7 Very rarely will anyone die for a righteous man, though for a good man someone might possibly dare to die. 8 But God demonstrates his own love for us in this: While we were still sinners, Christ died for us."*NIV

Romans 5:6-8 *"For when we were yet without strength, in due time Christ died for the ungodly. 7 For scarcely for a righteous man will one die: yet peradventure for a good man some would even dare to die. 8 But God commendeth His love toward us, in that, while we were yet sinners, Christ died for us.'"* KJV

John 17:11 Jesus prays for each of us: *"I will remain in the world no longer, but they* **(we who are on this earth at this moment)** *are still in the world, and I am coming to You. Holy Father, protect them by the power of Your name—the Name You gave me—so that they may be one as we are one."* (From the Intercessory prayer of Jesus, John 17)

Individuals are to live, humbly . . . seeking to be faithful unto God, giving thanks in their daily walk with God—aware of the fact of sin in our lives, for all have sinned and come short of the glory of God. **Romans 3:22** *"This righteousness from God comes through faith in Jesus Christ to all who believe. There is no difference, 23 for all have sinned and fall short of the glory of God, 24 and are justified freely by his grace through the redemption that came by Christ Jesus. 25 God presented him as a sacrifice of atonement, through faith in his blood. He did this to demonstrate his justice, because in his forbearance he had left the sins committed beforehand unpunished."* NIV

APPEALING TO THE YOUTH

Dr. Edie writes: (Pilgrim Press, 2007) "We tend to ask, 'How can we make worship more appealing to our youth? rather than, **How can we ensure that youth will encounter the fullness of the presence of the living God in worship?**'" Think realistically about this. It basically goes back to family and home life. There is little we can do to make up for the lack of family life! Everything else is simply a Band-Aid. Until our youth actually have a family life, where parents and family are truly respected, and come to worship as a family, we are at a loss as to what to try next to gain the interest of our young people!!!

We have heard it over and over again that we must have contemporary services to interest our young people, and get them to church. We have actually come to believe it. We may get youth to the church, and this is a fine beginning, but without **Biblical Worship,** very little that is lasting will happen, with the exception of a few happy memories. Tragically, self worship is a reality that must be dealt with, especially in this day and age. There are no funny stories, heroes, gimmicks, games, or comedian pastors, that can take the place of Biblical Worship. The Lord expects and desires true respect from all of us.

Family life has become minimized, because each member is heavily involved in different activities. Sometimes families, in an attempt to achieve some sort of oneness and togetherness, become so heavily involved in sporting activities which they enjoy, that there is no, or very little time left for corporate worship in the church of their choice. I often think of the time we invited a young 11 year old neighbor boy to go with us to Sunday School and worship. He was so sincere in his response, when he said: "I know I should be in church, but I am just so busy!" Where did he get this idea?

What do youth want in a worship service? They are still growing and learning, therefore in their tender years they aren't prepared to say for sure what they need or want in worship. They will find the answer in time, but for now, they should patiently follow the example of their elders. They do not know enough about God to come up with an answer for worship that is theologically (Biblically) correct. They know how to plan programs, and entertainment, but this is not worship. We had better be asking "What does God want from *all of us* as we gather for corporate worship?" In our worship God wants us to praise Him in silence, enabling all worshipers present to hear His voice, and then leave the worship experience having been inspired, informed, and fitted for service. "The Family that worships together and prays together, stays together." Corporate worship is not a program. We all have room to grow in the worship experience. You may come to worship as you are . . . but never be content to stay as you are! The worship of the Lord God is a learning, growing and precious experience. It is a time of yielding to God our Savior who is present! *"The Lord is in His holy temple, let all the earth keep silence before Him!"* (Habakkuk 2:20)

Young people are being programmed by the endless daily activities to which they are exposed. Young people may think they know what they want and need, but have little idea what life is going to throw at them. How differently life can turn out, from one's youthful dreams! The days of our youth are filled with youthful thoughts and plans. Young people need to be led and taught by experienced Godly parents and other Christian adults. They are young persons under construction. The learning process is often slow and boring to a young person! When you look at little children, they are so uninhibited: they call things as they see them.

Look at **Matthew 18:1-5** *"At that time the disciples came to Jesus and asked, "Who is the greatest in the kingdom of heaven?"* **2** *He called a little child and had him stand among them.* **3** *And he said: "I tell you the truth, unless you change and become like little children, you will never enter the kingdom of heaven.* **4** *Therefore, whoever humbles himself like this child is the greatest in the kingdom of heaven."* **5 And whoso shall receive one such little child in my name receiveth me.** *"*

These little ones are so dependent upon Mom and Dad. Parents are the only god these little ones know at that point in their lives. This is why parents, and all adults, need the humble qualities of a child.

APPEALING TO ALL AGES

When at corporate worship, one cannot worship <u>for</u> someone else. Worship is a very personal experience between the individual and God. Every individual must surrender to God, and receive the inspiration of God's presence in Christ. God is present! The worship experience is not a time to have one's cell phone turned on, and not the time to listen to an I-Pod, for playing games, or sending text messages! We attend corporate worship for the inspiration we need to be motivated, and then go out to live for Christ. This inspiration is to be found in the *conscious realization that God is present,* as He has promised he would be—as recorded in **Matthew 18:20** *"Where two or three are gathered together in my name, there I am in the midst of them."* The Lord is present in the hearing and reading of God's Word; in the sermon as it is preached; and, in the fellowship with others who are at worship and receiving the same inspiration you are experiencing! This is true unity! We are the body of Christ on earth! He has no other hands but ours!

Until families begin to worship together <u>as a family</u>, we will keep loosing our youth. Young people think their life is long, and its end is so far away. Young people today are exposed to everything imaginable and more! They are concentrating on the here and now: living for the moment. This makes it very difficult for youth to give much serious consideration about their future. Most young people have tried, seen, and done everything; by the time they are in their early teens. Therefore many become bored. To find newness, and thrills, so many of our young people experiment with pre-marital sex, drugs, and you name it! It is easy for youth to put off their turning to God, and to have the desire to attend corporate worship in order to praise God from Whom all blessings flow. Fortunately, there is a remnant of fine young people. These are made up of youth who have accepted Jesus, along with God's Word, while they were quite young! Their lives give testimony and praise to God. When a young person accepts Jesus Christ as Lord and Savior, his or her life is changed forever. They are forgiven and forgiving sinners. **Romans 12:9** *"Let love be without dissimulation. Abhor (hate) that which is evil; cleave (hang on) to that which is good."*

Young people, do NOT attempt to mold your lives by yielding to what everyone else is doing, just to be popular.

Are we really ever finished with *construction* in our lives? We never reach what we think of, when speaking about perfection. In worship we come before our Creator, whom we call God . . . and He alone is worth-worshiping. A common error has been to suppose that rituals have some value, regardless of the attitude of the heart. Worship is a conscious glorification of God growing out off the inner attitude of a humble heart that is submitting to God's authority and purpose for that life. Scripture calls all people to worship God. **Revelation 14:6,7** *"Then I saw another angel flying in the midst of heaven, having the everlasting gospel to preach to those who dwell on the earth—to every nation, tribe, tongue, and people—7 saying with a loud voice, 'Fear God and give glory to Him, for the hour of His judgment has come; and worship Him who made heaven and earth, the sea and springs of water'"* KJV

We get out of worship just what we put into it. If the service is boring, are we boring? Don't expect worship to be a source of entertainment, but it should be a source of inspiration. This in itself will keep free from boredom. Worship is a time of total, humble, and sincere, openness to God. At worship a person is like a vessel waiting to be filled with the blessings of the Lord through His Word. God wants to speak to us, as he did to Isaiah in **Isaiah chapter 6**, which tells about Isaiah's call into the service of the Lord. We all need to feel God's call! (See Isaiah's Call, Page 38)

When we enter the sanctuary we must never loose sight of *The Great I Am*—GOD. We are in church to worship (regardless of our age). That in and of itself will end boredom at worship! If we come to worship expecting to be entertained; rather than inspired, motivated, and equipped to serve God more faithfully, we will be bored.

THE SABBATH AND THE LORD'S DAY

Corporate worship is really an outgrowth of the Ten Commandments. **Exodus 20:8-11** reads: *Remember the sabbath day, to keep it holy. 9 Six days shalt thou labour, and do all thy work: 10 But the seventh day is the sabbath of the LORD thy God: in it thou shalt not do any work, thou, nor thy son, nor thy daughter, thy manservant, nor thy maidservant, nor thy cattle, nor thy stranger that is within thy gates. 11 For in six days the LORD made heaven and earth, the sea, and all that in them is, and rested the seventh day:"*

Having finished His creation, God rested on the 7th day of the week (Saturday), and has commanded that we humans also rest on this day. After the resurrection of Christ, however, the early Apostles and early Christians assembled themselves together on The Lord's Day, in honor of Christ's resurrection. This became their day of rest and renewal. Scripture tells us: **Acts 20:7** *"And upon the first day of the week, when the disciples came together to break bread, Paul preached unto them,* ready to depart on the_morrow; *and continued his speech until midnight."* Some think this was a one time event out of respect for Paul, who was leaving the next day.

Some are bound to say "We don't keep the Sabbath, because that is for Jews, and for another time . . . right?—wrong! We are still bound by the Word of God to keep the Sabbath day holy! Think about this: we would still be observing the Sabbath Day if God had not sent His Son as the Lamb of God, to take away the sin of the world. We have been redeemed, and saved from our sin and have been granted a pardon from the death sentence, which we really do not deserve. That's why we call it GRACE. This is where grace comes into play! Jesus rose from the dead on Sunday

In Mark's gospel **2:27** we read *"The Sabbath was made for man, not man for the Sabbath."* KJV In other words, Man needs one day out of seven to rest, and the Lord God has given us this example: God rested on the 7th day. God, our Creator knew that Man needed a day for rest and refreshment from the usual daily tasks.

Hebrews 10:25 *"Not forsaking the assembling of ourselves together, as the manner of some is; but exhorting one another: and so much the more, as ye see the day approaching."* KJV

Isaiah 45:20 *"Gather together and come; assemble, you fugitives from the nations. Ignorant are those who carry about idols of wood, who pray to gods that cannot save."* NIV

Looking again at **Mark 2:27** above . . . since the Sabbath was made for man and not man for the Sabbath, it is appropriate that most mainline churches observe *"The Lord's Day"* as their day of rest in honor of Christ's resurrection.

We can worship God most everywhere, and this is true. However, **the Sunday Corporate Worship** experience is in keeping with what the disciples of Christ did after Christ's resurrection. We have all heard of persons who try to convince us, that they can worship God on the golf course, or on a fishing boat, or at a sports event, etc. Yes, you should worship God and praise Him wherever you may be. But, **The Lord's Day** is **Special** and set apart (*Holy*) from all other days of the week. At the same time also keep in mind, that **all creation gives praise to the Lord** every day of the week. Let us remember that each Sunday we are celebrating Easter again as we worship!

It is interesting to learn there are 540 churches who, still observe Saturday as their Sabbath and day of rest. (Here is the web site to type into your browser if you want to see the list):

(http://www.the-ten-commandments.org/sabbathkeepingchurches.html)

We are familiar with some of these churches that observe the Sabbath of the Old Testament: The Seventh Day Adventists, The Church of Christ, The World Wide Church of God, and The Seventh day Baptist Church of Christ, and the list continues.

In this day of technology, and labor savings devices, persons are finding they don't have enough time for all their plans. The reason is that we take on too much: we are too busy. We often find ourselves multitasking (doing two or more things at the same time). We use Sunday as the day to catch up on what we didn't have time to do during the week.

It has been said, "If you want to destroy Christianity, get rid of their Sabbath, or The Lord's Day." Be it well known from this point on . . . the devil knows just how to annihilate Christianity. satan or the devil; can always tempt you with something that will keep you so busy, you won't have time to worship God publicly at corporate worship! Destroy the Lord's Day Sabbath, and the Church will die a slow death. Without dedicated planned fellowship, there isn't an organization on earth that could exist, or last very long. The fact is, we need each other, no matter with what group we may affiliate!

When Christians gather together for corporate worship, they are witnessing to the community, and to the world, that they are putting their trust in God and His plan of salvation. We know there is no other way to be saved. **Acts 4:12** *"Neither is there salvation in any other: for there is none other name under heaven given among men, whereby we must be saved."* KJV

We gather for worship to express our gratitude to the Lord for all He has given us! We also gather for inspiration, instruction, and prayer. If there is no time to keep the Sabbath day holy, then we are too busy, and we need to recognize this as a fact, and do something to make the necessary changes! The only real reasons for missing the corporate worship experiences are illness; some form of incapacitation; or, for and honest legitimate reason known to you. Worship is not something we decide to do each Lord's Day: it is something we do!

PARENTS: THE CAUSE AND THE CURE

For further consideration: It wasn't so many years ago, perhaps 60 or more, when clothiers made clothing to suit the adult world in general. There were no designer jeans for the young men and women of that day. Through the years, ever so subtly, things have changed. Now it is the teen-age generation to whom the clothing industry directs much of its efforts. Why? The answer is simple—money! Some schools have a special dress code for their students. It is no longer acceptable for girls to wear plunging necklines and short mini skirts to school, and the boys are not to wear those low crotch baggy pants. It is difficult to understand why parents are up in arms over dress codes. Some schools have gone so far as to have their students were uniforms, and this seems to be a fine answer to some of their problems.

Parents should also realize that much of the cultural life style of today has had a deadening impact on our churches, and how we visualize worship to be.

Also, we have the mistaken notion that the mega-churches have everything worked out right; therefore we should do as they do, because they are drawing in the crowds. Does this mean they are doing things right? Not all BIG churches are worshiping in a manner that is pleasing to God. Televangelism often does more harm for the Church, than good. Many of these televangelists claim they are anointed by God. Next, they ask their listeners to sow *seed money* (send money to them). The implication is that if they send *seed money* their financial situation will be taken care of by the Lord.

Unlike Job, we are not blameless, so let us clean up our act, and worship the Lord in Spirit and in Truth. Christians need to shed themselves of the desire to come into the House of the Lord with their own ideas and whims. We have promoted *our way* long enough. Let us all calm down in our churches and behave like believers in Christ. Frank Sinatra sang a popular song about how many worship when he put these words to music:

"I DID IT MY WAY"

*And now the end is near, and so I face the final curtain, my friend I'll say it clear . . . I'll state my case of which I am certain. I've lived a life that's full. I traveled each and every high-way. And more, much more than this, **I did it my way**. Regrets? I've had a few, But then again too few to mention. I did what I had to do. And saw it through without exemption. I planned each charted course . . . Each careful step along the byway, and more, much more than this **I did it my way**. Yes there were times I'm sure you knew. When I bit off more than I could chew . . . But through it all when there was doubt I ate it up and spit it out, I faced it all . . . and stood tall and **did it my way**. I've loved, I've laughed and cried . . . I've had my fill, my share of losing. And now as tears subside I find it all so amusing. To think I did all that, and may I say not in a shy way . . . Oh no, oh no, not me. **I did it my way**. For what is a man what has he got, if not himself then he has not. To say the things he truly feels and not the words of one who kneels. The record shows I took the blows . . . and **did it my way**.*

There are many in churches who want things done their way?

A WORD TO PARENTS

Young people need to respect adults, and they also need adults to respect them: although they may not realize it at the time. Youth really want loving discipline and sound training. They need to know we love them, and the best way to show this is to say **"no"** sometimes. In my first church I had a very large Sunday School class of 22 learners, all of high school age. One young lad was constantly causing problems. He had to be called on the proverbial carpet quite often. Another young man in my class (Ralph) said to me, "You don't like me as much as you do Craig do you?" I asked him why he made such a statement. He responded, "Because you are always getting after Craig when he does something wrong or questionable."

Without question, young people need and want to be supervised, corrected, respected, disciplined and loved. I repeat this phrase quite often I know, but here it is again anyway. **We have to stand for something, or we will fall for anything.** This is our witness to the world and community! We must stand upon the solid rock of Christ, or we will fall for anything that wets our appetites. **Ephesians 4:14 and 15**—speaks to this most emphatically: *"That we henceforth be no more children, tossed to and fro, and carried about with every wind of doctrine, by the sleight of men, and cunning craftiness, whereby they lie in wait to deceive;* 15 *But speaking the truth in love, may grow up into him in all things, which is the head, even Christ:"* KJV

Saying **"yes"** and providing every want for your child is not the answer; and, it definitely is not the way to solve problems within the Church. So much of what we do at the local church level, may be compared to a **vaccine,** or an **inoculation.** We get just enough of God, Christ, and the Bible, (the real thing in small amounts) to immune youth and older persons against the real Christ, and the leading of His Holy Spirit, for the remainder of their lives. The real thing is to "Walk your talk!" Christ and His Church must come first before all else in our life! We need to rethink our premises! *The Church is the body of Christ, for heaven's sake.*

Our youth need parents who set the example, and **come as a family to worship Almighty God.** Throughout my ministry, I have witnessed an endless chain of well meaning parents who bring their children to Sunday School; only to drop them off, and come later to pick them up again. What is this teaching their children? We have all heard young people say, "When I get older, I won't have to go to Sunday School! After all Sunday School is for kids!"

Think about this: how many who attend corporate worship, also attend Sunday School? The answer is very few. Yet, Sunday School is the same as Bible study for all ages. If a person doesn't have time to take one hour or two out of his or her busy schedule each week, to attend corporate worship and Sunday School, it would be well to re-evaluate one's Christian walk.

Sunday school allows for dialogue between the class members and the teacher. In this setting we share our faith experiences with others as the Word of God is studied and applied to life.

Attending corporate worship and Sunday School is *our response to having already accepted God and His plan for our lives.* When we attend Sunday School, we are, in essence, saying we don't know all we should about the Word of God, but we are trying to learn more!

We need to change our concepts as to how persons are converted to Christ. A person's acceptance of Christ as Lord and Savior, begins in the home, where parents love, and honor God, through the use of Scripture, prayer and service to others. Many pastors preach salvation messages: to help save souls through their sermon. The sermon is for instruction, correction, inspiration, and growth—for the persons who have already heard of God in their home environment, as well as for those who do not have the background of godly parents. The prime responsibility is **in the home, under the guidance of The Holy Spirit.** This is why God ordained marriage and family life. It is God's intent, that through family living children would come to know God's plan of salvation through Christ. Unfortunately, there are numerous homes in today's life style of living, where the only way children will hear the name of God is through the endless curse words heard. No matter how financially poor a family may be, there is no excuse for not properly training a child in the way that he or she should go. Poverty is not a sin!

Fortunately, many do come to Christ in spite of their home life. Perhaps you, or the pastor, or even an unrealized experience, may have been the motivation for a person to repent, then turn to Christ, and experience salvation for themselves. Mostly, however, a person comes to worship, because he or she has already experienced, and responded to their need for a closer walk with the Lord. The work of the Holy Spirit is to convict persons of their sin and their need. From that point, the desire to worship and praise the Lord with others of like faith, becomes a part of their life. This binds them together, much as was the case with the early disciples after the resurrection. They wanted to worship because they already knew of Christ. "Blest Be the Tie that Binds." is another hymn of truth.

The solitary task of Jesus was to be about His Father's business that we might be saved. Worship is that point in our experience, where we appropriately honor and glorify God, for all He has made possible for us in this life on earth, within the fellowship of believers. However, church going must not be the sum total of one's Christian experience! We are on this testing ground, called earth, for such a short time! We have been created to do good works, that the Father may be glorified. **Matthew 5:16** *"Let your light so shine before men, that they may see your good works, and glorify your Father which is in heaven."*

Youthful activities may get our youth to the church, and this seems to be the goal these days. We agree that it may get youth to the church, where they need to be for exposure to true Christianity, and where they may learn and grow along with their friends. This is the goal . . . the beginning; but, we need to keep a keen eye of the end result! We need to be firmly planted upon the reason we are the Church. The Church is Christ's Body on earth, (and we are His hands). The Church is not a building, or club trying to satisfy everyone's appetites. Our goal is to reach out to persons so they will repent of sin and accept Jesus Christ as their personal Lord and Savior. This is much more important than any extra curricular activity!

What our youth need is not more games, and hyper music, but the joy of the real Christ in their hearts! If the church needs sports and contemporary music to keep youth interested in the church, something is drastically inaccurate with the Church's message! The *Fellowship of Christian Athletes* gives a fine witness to the Lord, but idolizing these athletes is not the same as you being a Christian yourself. You may dress up in a policeman's uniform, but that does not make you a policeman.

123

Ecclesiastes 11:9 *"Be happy, young man, while you are young, and let your heart give you joy in the days of your youth. Follow the ways of your heart and whatever our eyes see, but know that in all these things God will bring you to judgment."* NIV We are answerable to God, not our peers!

Youth meetings are an excellent time to teach the Word of God. Only those who are caught up in the ways of the world find learning about God boring. The Lord God speaks in a still small voice, yet we want dramatic, neurotic, loud and offbeat exhibitions to keep us alert and satisfied. Remember it is God who has given you everything that you think you possess. Think about it—all good and perfect gifts come from God and belong to God. **Luke 11:13** *"If you then, though you are evil, know how to give good gifts to our children, how much more will your Father in heaven give the Holy Spirit to those who ask him!"*

RITUALS

Parents and youth alike need to give responsible attention to how they answer specific questions within the rituals of the church. At Dedications, Baptisms, Weddings, Confirmation, Church membership, etc., it is so easy to answer "I will, or I do" or "We will or we do" . . . when responding to the pastor's questions from the ritual. We know we cannot say "no", to these questions in our rituals, for this would end the ceremony. Sad but true, we have made promises after promises that mean nothing more than a ceremonial gimmick to many. *"Your ego is writing checks your body cannot or will not cash."* So many cannot keep the vows they make from the ritual.

We are living under a false sense of security; often uncertain about our personal salvation. You can be confident in your salutation because God does not lie. **John 11:25,26** *"Jesus said unto her* (**Martha**), *I am the resurrection, and the life: he that believeth in me, though he were dead, yet shall he live: 26 And whosoever liveth and believeth in me* *shall never die. Believest thou this?"* **Acts 16:31** *"And they* **(Paul and Silas)** *said, Believe on the Lord Jesus Christ, and thou shalt be saved, and thy house."*

1 John 5:13 *"These things I have written to you who believe in the name of the Son of God, in order that you may know that you have eternal life"*

Salvation is not automatic. You have to do something first: Believe, Repent, and Accept. Salvation is a free gift from the Lord, and all one has to do is repent and accept Gods' offer for eternal life. There is really nothing you can do by way of works to earn salvation. This is why salvation is based upon the grace (unearned favor) of God. Being saved however does mean that you will want do the good works you were created to do.

The one key element to confidence in the individual's salvation is based upon the promises of God, who does not lie. Any other attempts at personal salvation is likened to an individual who tries to bake a cake without baking powder! It will not turn out right! Beware of false security. I shall never forget asking my mother, when I was around 10 years of age, "If I were to die, would I got to heaven." She responded, "Well, you were baptized." There you have the beginnings of a good old false sense of security! That is not the answer I should have gotten, or really needed! Baptism is not an insurance policy guaranteeing salvation! Baptism is our response to God's Word.

<u>YOUTH MINISTRY</u>

Much of our present day *youth ministry,* is directed toward programs and activities for fun and fellowship. Youth need to be part of a ministry where they may they may bear witness to their personal experience with Christ. Give them something constructive to do in the church, so they will feel needed, and where results can be seen. Church choirs (vocal, bell or instrumental) are excellent ways to involve youth. Let them usher, light the candles, and more important, let them be part of the church united . . . not divided by the contemporary/ traditional concept of worship. We are one church: not two churches meeting in the same building. Youth ministry should be focused around *the wisdom of the Church's most sacred practices:* **Preaching the Word of God in Scripture**, **Holy Communion**, the **Baptism of believers**, along with solemn moments of **Prayer**. This is critical to a person's experiencing an encounter with God. And yes . . . we do need encounters with God, in and outside the home: In fact everywhere we go. Not all worship takes place in the church building. This is what worship is—**AN ENCOUNTER WITH THE LORD, THAT LEADS TO INSPIRATION, AND INSPIRATION LEADS TO MOTIVATION AND MOTIVATION LEADS TO ACTION AND ACTION LEADS TO A SATISFYING LIFE OF SERVING THE LORD IN EVERYTHING A PERSON DOES.** Always remember: **We are created to do good works.**

Ephesians 2:8-9 *"For it is by grace you have been saved, through faith—and this not from yourselves, it is the gift of God—9 not by works, so that no one can boast. 10 For we are God's workmanship, created in Christ Jesus to do good works, which God prepared in advance for us to do."* NIV

This leads to an encounter with the world in which one lives, but at the same time, also know that we are not of this world. Youth and adults should realize this important distinction as well. **John 17:14** *"I have given them thy word; and the world hath hated them, because they are not of the world, even as I am not of the world."* KJV Don't be afraid to talk to youth . . . they will not bite!

THE DEFINITION OF MUSIC

Music has been defined as an ART, *the art of arranging sounds in time so as to produce a continuous, unified, and evocative composition,* *as through melody, harmony, rhythm, and timbre. Also, music is an aesthetically pleasing or harmonious sound or combination of sounds. Worship should accomplish much the same as we praise and worship the Lord, i.e., in unity and harmony. Anything other than this is noise, such as the scratching of one's fingernail on the blackboard. Worshipful Music must <u>inspire</u>, <u>entertain</u>, <u>calm one's spirit</u>, and <u>bring with it the sense of joy</u>, <u>well-being and peace</u>. Music makes one feel good! Indeed, music <u>sooths</u> the savage beast in all of us. Music is made up of Harmonious sounds through various arrangements that create beauty, joy, a calm spirit, and peace.*

Music **used for worship** should not call attention to the person (singing or playing an instrument), for they are **doing their best to praise the Lord through their efforts.** One needs to dethrone self in order to worship God, Who is high and lifted up (**Isaiah 6:1**). At corporate worship services, **all performances to the glory of self, are out of place.** We need to test ourselves to see if we are worshiping and glorifying God, or some person/s who is/are **up front** being seen and admired. Instead, one should thank God for the talent the soloist (vocalist or instrumentalist) has been given. It doesn't take applause to let the performer know they are much appreciated. If music is for entertainment, we applaud. <u>If our music is for the praise and worship of God, then applause is out of place.</u> <u>The sounds of applause interfere with, and break the spirit of inspiration and oneness with the Lord, which the worship service has led up to, at that point and time</u>. The best compliment one can pay the individual, choir or group, is silence when they have finished, for this lets the individual or group know they have touched and inspired the hearts of the congregation. Applauding when children are part of the worship is fine; they need encouragement, but as they grow older, they soon learn the meaning and purpose of worship, and not be offended if there is no clapping of hands when they have been praising the Lord with their God given talent! There are times when silence is golden.

We must begin to make wise choices in the music we use at worship, or we are left with endless sounds that have nothing to do with worshipful music. With an open, intellectual and honest mind, please consider the endless other sounds that really have nothing to do with music. The sounds and antics coming from *KISS*, *Judas Priest*, *AC/DC*, *The Rolling Stones*, and others like them, are endless! Their sounds are indescribably disturbing; and, this list goes on and on in the entertainment world of today! In some of these performers the mainliner hops widely across the stages of the world, dressed in unseemly, and grotesque wear, along with devilish makeup. **It is a sad commentary on the morals of America, and the World, when the majority of people are calling these sounds music!** IT IS NOT MUSIC! Rather . . . it is Sinai being lived all over again. (See what happened at Sinai, page 9).

There are several television stations wholly dedicated to music videos, that are laden with depravity. As writer of this material, I can only come to the conclusion that satan is real, if one needs further proof! Certainly, there is nothing inspiring about these sounds, antics, or demonstrations endured to produce such noise. I suppose if I were being raised in today's world, as a young person, I would be following some of these same trends: doing what everyone else is doing . . . **if** I had not accepted God's plan of salvation in the Savior Jesus Christ. Our main difficulty is that there is really very little else out there, in the mainstream of entertainment, that is offering anything better! This depicts the satanic downward trend of a world, that no longer accepts God and Jesus Christ the Savior. Fortunately, *Jesus is the Savior.* But, for now, satan is the god of this world, and knows that his time is indeed short! Look at **Revelation 12:12** ***"Therefore rejoice, the heavens, and you that dwell in them. Woe unto the inhabitants of the earth and of the sea for the devil is cone down to you, having great wrath, because*** <u>***he knows that his time is short.***</u>***"***

What is being written herein, has absolutely nothing to do with what many will call *"Age Related."* That is a **huge** '<u>**copout**</u>.' Truth remains the same for all ages. All we do and say, at any age, must be in alignment with the Word of God in Scripture! Some of the music of the Big Bands of the 40's was not all great and fitting either. Although the big bands did have arrangements to follow, and harmony: blends of sound. Many of the words were not always appropriate. We all have our various likes, for one reason or another: our upbringing; but, there is great music in the world, if one will but take the time to learn to enjoy something new. Please look at the section on <u>Much Secular Music Comes From the Classics</u>, for better understanding of what is being said here. (see page 76)

I am always surprised, inspired, and amazed, when a young person elevates his or her goals, and is learning to play music . . . other than what their peers may be playing and enjoying: music from the great composers. These young people most likely have ***discerning parents,*** since this is where their attitudes concerning life begin. Every human being begins his or her life as an "**empty vessel**." After all "<u>Home is where your story begins</u>." That young vessel is going to be filled: no getting around that! What is being put into the young human vessel determines what the child is becoming! If youth are not being filled with proper values by their parent/s, along with the proper worship of their Creator: they will get these values from another source: the street, friends, television, the media, or the movies they watch! If you haven't yet come to this conclusion, please know that Hollywood has! Hollywood makes the claim that their movies are depicting the real world. What Hollywood does not want to understand, or admit, is that movies are great object lessons for teaching. Movies shape the world's values, actions and manner of speech. Hollywood also knows that religion and sex sells, and money dictates what they produce. What a shock it would be if our forefathers could come back to see what Hollywood is turning out as movies these days, along with what is on television.

THE ORGAN USED FOR WORSHIP?

It must be admitted that many churches do not have an organ, or if they do, quite often, especially in small town churches, there is no one who can play it. Not many are taking organ lessons these days. Even in Europe we are told some of those great organs are not being cared for, and the result is they are deteriorating slowly but surely. What does this tell us?

Sometimes we have to do the best we can with what we have. In Austria, there was a small church, where the Christmas carol "Silent Night" was born. In 1818, a small band of traveling actors were performing in some of the small towns of the Austrian Alps. On December 23, they arrived at Bergdorf, a village near Salzburg where they were to perform the story of Christ's birth in the small church of St. Nicholas. Unfortunately the organ in this small church was not working, and would not be repaired in time for Christmas. Thinking of the Christmas story, pastor Mohr was inspired to write the words to Silent Night, but he needed a melody to go with it. So he went to visit with the church organist, Franz Xavier Gruber. He had only a few hours to come up with the melody, and it was performed that night with a singing congregation and Gruber's guitar. And we all know that *Silent Night* has become one of the most beloved Christmas carols of all time. If this is all you have, or if a piano is all the church has, this is fine! Use what talent is available.

In cases of the unexpected, we may need to improvise. We have been blessed with great inspirational music and regardless of the instrument/s we may have at our disposal, we should sing to the glory of the Lord. We could even sing without accompaniment, i.e., A-Cappella.

Pipe organs existed throughout the ancient world, although they were quite different from the organs of the sixtieth century and later, which are the organs familiar to us today.

What we need to stress here, is that **the organ** used for the worship of God has withstood the test of time throughout generations, **until**

today. Organ music combines an entire orchestra of sounds, and therefore was the perfect instrument used with which to glorify God. The Organ has been described as *The voice of God* (Andrew Unsworth Mormon Tabernacle Organist) and *The Harmony of Heaven* (Clay Christianson Mormon Tabernacle Organist). The Bible mentions various instruments—the harp; organ; ram's horn; cymbals; trumpets; cornet; stringed instruments; dulcimer; flute, and then of course the human voice (singers). With music we worship the Lord. Music reaches the soul of a person, in a way the spoken word cannot. And take note that in many churches, the organist is not visible to the congregation, or at least is not *up there* performing, as before an audience. The organist is leading the congregational singing. We always need to be on guard against performing for personal glorification! Worship is not about the worship leader: worship is all about God and giving Him all the glory. All God asks of us is that we take time in our worldly endeavors to *be still in order to know Him.*

INSTRUMENTS IN WORSHIP

The use of instruments in the worship of God is seen throughout Scripture. The Mormon Tabernacle Choir is accompanied by a symphony orchestra (and organ) that is second to none! This choir has been called America's Choir. Concordia College (Missouri Synod Lutheran) has a tremendous music program, blending a perfectly toned orchestra with a choir to praise God. There are many others of course, but I am only giving two examples. We may not have the wherewithal to make such beautiful music, however, some of the most inspirational music I have ever heard came from sincere Christian worshipers, as they praise the Lord with what ever talent and ability they may have. If all one has is a guitar to accompany a soloist, this can be of great inspiration, if the proper music is selected and performed with dignity to the glory of God!

We are all walking on sacred ground! Let us walk with humble spirits and faith filled hearts. If we have all the necessary gifts, but one thing is lacking: then we are useless . . . remember! I Corinthians 13:1 ***"Though I speak with the tongues of men and of angels, and <u>have not</u> <u>love</u>, I am become as <u>noisy</u> <u>brass</u>, or a <u>clanging</u> <u>cymbal</u>."***

Music and *gladness* calms our turbulent life . . . giving our hearts a sense of worship and deep joy; which pride can never do. **Proverbs 16:18** ***"Pride goeth before destruction, and a haughty spirit before a fall."***

When we do gather for worship in the church, we enter His gates with *thanksgiving*: then we can heartily, joyfully, and meaningfully sing songs of praise. The words we hear and sing in the hymns, not only inspire us, but teach us as well from the experiences of the composer: which may well have been similar to our own experiences. This brings the thoughtful worshiper indescribable deep joy, calmness and inspiration. Obedience also brings peace and joy to the soul. And we are truly *thankful* because God has met all our needs through Jesus Christ. Yes . . . we are to make a *joyful noise* unto the Lord, as Wesley instructs: **"<u>Be no more afraid of your voice now, nor more ashamed of its being heard, than when you sung the songs of satan.</u>"**

DID JOHN WESLEY, OR MARTIN LUTHER USE MUSIC FROM THE BARS AND SECULAR MUSIC OF THEIR DAY?

If you were raised in darkest Africa, the music of that culture is what you would call your music of choice! That would be the sum total of your exposure to music. The background for much of this kind of music comes out of their worship of idols and/or other gods. Is it proper to put Christian words to this type of music, and then use it for the worship of God?

It has been said that John Wesley used music from the bars of his time: the familiar tunes; for people to sing praises to the Lord. This is a popular misconception that continues to survive among United Methodists: that John and Charles Wesley made use of the popular melodies of their day: tavern, drinking, or bar songs, with new and appropriate words for their hymns. This sounds logical. After all, these worldly tunes were familiar to the masses. The same is often said of the great reformer and musician, Martin Luther. This claim is sometimes made to show the extent of their evangelistic zeal; namely, that they would go out into the secular culture, even into the taverns, saloons, and parlors frequented by the sinners they sought to redeem, and made use of their musical language, the familiar drinking song tunes, for their own sacred hymns. This claim continues to be made today by some musicians, pastors, worship leaders, composers and hymn writers. **Unfortunately, this is not true. It is a misapplication of a historical inaccuracy.**

Dean McIntyre, director of music resources at the Board of Discipleship of the United Methodist Church, confesses his experiences when he said, "I have been an agent of misinformation. Over the years, I have repeated the story that Charles and John Wesley used the tunes of drinking songs for some of their hymns. Like most people who said this, <u>I was encouraging people to be open to "secular" influences in church music</u>. I was not lying; lying means knowingly telling a falsehood. I was simply repeating a statement that I had heard and read from several sources. I now know that my sources were misinformed." (Used by Permission)

"The truth is that the music of the Wesley's and that of Martin Luther never made such use of saloon songs, nor would they have condoned such use! There is also the deeper issue of whether the importing of secular and drinking songs into the church to accompany congregational singing would be acceptable to the Wesley." Wesley issued three collections of tunes: **(1)** the *Founder Collection* in 1742, **(2)** *Select Hymns with Tunes Annex* in 1761, (in which first appears his celebrated 'Directions for Singing,' which are reprinted on page 7 of *The United Methodist Hymnal*), and **(3)** his last, *Sacred Harmony,* in

1780. What we find in these collections yields an important insight into Wesley's musical aesthetic for hymn tunes. Here we find the simple, traditional psalm tunes and hymn melodies, primarily from Anglican songs. John Wesley made use of _new tunes_ composed or adapted from _folk tunes_, _sacred and secular oratorio_, and even _operatic melodies_. It should not escape us that whenever Wesley allowed the use of secular music as from an oratorio or opera, he used music of accepted high standard and almost always from classical rather than popular sources. **In no instance did Wesley turn to tavern or drinking songs or other such unseemly sources to carry the sacred texts of songs and hymns."** (Taken from Dean McIntyre's website:

http://www.gbod.org/site/apps/nlnet/content3.aspx?c=nhLRJ2PM KsG&b=5713093&ct=3842051)

If Wesley's reasoning for the Methodists of his time remains valid for our generation (even though centuries have intervened), then we must confess we are missing the mark. When we ignore tradition, we soon loose our direction. Those who choose to use such worldly music in worship should be able to dispute Wesley's practice convincingly. **Furthermore, those who justify, in our day, the use of secular culture and influences in United Methodist worship, by claiming that Wesley used drinking songs in his own day should be called to account.**

But someone has said, "Must we base our thoughts of worship way back to Wesley's time, and how it was done then? Isn't anything new acceptable?" Yes, there is a great deal of new and inspirational beautiful Christian music being composed today that is acceptable. However, there is far too much new and shallow music, with repetitious words that claim to know what God is like, and that tell God what He is like. This is not acceptable! God knows what He is like, and what He requires of us! Churches today are being divided over the music we use at worship. Music that invokes pride and body movements is very questionable for use in worship the Lord our God. We do not come to worship to demonstrate how *spiritual we are* by calling attention to ourselves through body language. Many churches do not see this as a problem that is dividing us. satan knows just how to inactivate a church's witness to the world. Divisions over how to worship are all too common today! Now we have congregations made up of elderly people, and another made up largely of younger people: worshiping separately. People want to worship the Lord and do it *their way*. Something is drastically wrong if we Christians cannot worship together! Age should not be a dividing factor.

Mega churches *appear* to be doing very well today. People of all ages like to be where the action is, where things are happening, and where their friends are attending! We need to honestly ask: "Is the 'contemporary style' of worship the reason people are attending a certain church?"

We visited Hope Lutheran in Des Moines, that has at least 7,000 members (So we have been told). We came away convinced that people are not attending that particular church because of its contemporary worship format; but, rather . . . and more importantly, they are coming because they are being fed from the Word of God! I made the comment on our way home, "I would like to go back again to hear another one of the pastor's Scriptural sermons, because they spoke to my needs." Nothing is more exciting than attending a church where God is truly glorified in a humble, manner, and where the needs of those in attendance are being met! Their flock has good reason to keep coming back for worship: not because the great hymns of the church are no longer being used by our standards. Lutheran hymnals have always been quite different from those of other denominations. Also, it must be admitted, the contemporary music being used at Hope Lutheran, honored the Lord with words of Scripture, without being repetitious, or theologically incorrect! Salvation by Grace, and not works, came through loud and clear!

In all denominations admittedly, there is always the possibility that people would come back to a certain church because of its programming.

In this case: just make sure that each Sunday you have a different show, gimmick, and/or something interesting to see.

Regardless of how the services are conducted, there is no reason or excuse for not using the great hymns of the church! Perhaps the problem is that we haven't the vaguest idea of <u>why</u> these great inspirational hymns were written. Therefore, to persons who are unfamiliar with these hymns, may find them boring, and the words a bit foreign. People will come to what is now labeled *traditional worship* just as readily as they come to the *contemporary worship* if they are being fed upon the Word of God and singing the great hymns of the church **with jest** and an understanding of what the composer meant when putting these words to music. Many times in my ministry, I would stop the congregational singing and ask, "Do you know what you are singing? Be alert and sing as though you believed the words you are singing, for they true, therefore they are inspiring, and you should feel the inspiration the writer felt as he wrote the hymn." We are all human, and are subject to the same needs, sorrows, joys, etc.

JOHN AND CHARLES WESLEY

Another help to understanding what Wesley considered appropriate in hymn tunes is to be found in his *"Directions for Singing,"* found on page VII of the United Methodist Hymnal. Of particular importance is a portion of his fourth direction: **"<u>Be no more afraid of your voice now, nor more ashamed of its being heard, than when you sung the songs of satan.</u>"** It is clear that Wesley intended that the "songs of satan" would and could not be used for public worship. Also important is his seventh direction: ***"Above all sing spiritually. Have an eye to God in every word you sing. <u>Aim at pleasing Him more than yourself, or any other creature.</u> In order to do this attend strictly to the sense of what you sing, and see that your heart is not carried away with the sound, but offered to God continually; so shall your singing be such*** *as the Lord will approve here, and reward you when He cometh in the clouds of heaven. Make a Joyful noise (sound) unto the Lord with whatever voice you may have."*

After the Wesley's conversion, John Wesley's brother Charles Wesley started writing hymns for the praise of God. Charles Wesley was sometimes called "the poet of Methodism," yet this designation really defined him too narrowly. He could more rightly be called the poet of Christianity, since his hymns have enjoyed such widespread use among various denominations. He wrote about 6,500 hymns, all of them after his conversion in 1738 and many of which are still popular. We know many, but just very few are mentioned here to get us started: *O For a Thousand Tongues to Sing; Hark! The Herald Angels Sing; Christ the Lord is Risen Today; Love Divine, All Loves Excelling; Soldiers of Christ Arise;* and, *Ye Servants of God.*

Today, the church is not at a loss for something to sing, and with which to praise God. We still have Christian composers who have experienced the Grace of God, and want to glorify God alone: not themselves. There is much contemporary music today that gives God the glory without that repetitive beat and the irritating heavy metal idiom.

Can anyone possibly think the great hymn *'Amazing Grace'* could ever be sung to the secular sounds heard today? The melody along with its words, have been called the most popular hymn of all time. It would be blasphemous to sing *Amazing Grace,* accompanied by the secular sounds of today. Admittedly, the bag pipe does it very well!

We belong to an electronically laden prosperous culture with plenty of food, and as recorded in **Luke 12:48** *"For unto whomsoever much is given, of him shall be much required."* KJV

OR

"From everyone who has been given much, much will be demanded; and from the one who has been entrusted with much, much more will be asked." NIV

We have been given much, and our *worship*, respect, and *gratitude* should be directed to God. We live in a land that is living in boredom, because we have had, and tried, everything imaginable. We are an *over-exposed* people. We are constantly trying new ways to keep people interested. The world calls it "marketing." Have you ever gone shopping at your favorite store because you know exactly where everything is. Ah . . . your item is not longer in its familiar spot: things have been moved to a new location. Why? The store manager wants you to shop around as you look for the item/s you know you need and want. In the meantime, you pick up things you may not need.

WHAT DOES THE LORD REQUIRE OF US?

The answer is very basic and simple, as quoted from Micah. 6:8. *"He hath shewed thee, O man, what is good; and what doth the LORD require of thee, but to do justly, and to love mercy, and to walk humbly with thy God?"* KJV

What is the plan of God for us? Simply this—to bring honor and glory to God in ALL things, and by Whom all things consist (hold together) as clearly stated in **Colossians 1:15** *The Son is the image of the invisible God, the firstborn over all creation. 16 For in him all things were created: things in heaven and on earth, visible and invisible, whether thrones or powers or rulers or authorities; all things have been created through him and for him. 17 He is before all things, and in him all things hold together."* KJV

It is sure a good thing we do not have to hold things together. We have created enough problems on our own, which by the way, we cannot fix. We can relax, knowing that God is in control!

God is not asking the impossible from us: only the respectable response due unto Him! He desires that we glorify Him, not ourselves! Remember Moses did not get to lead his people into the promised land because he just once took glory or credit unto

himself. **Numbers 20:10 reads:** *"And Moses and Aaron gathered the* *congregation together before the rock, and he said into them, Hear* *now ye rebels; must <u>we fetch</u> you water out of this rock?"* **Moses and** **Aaron didn't bring the water from the rock, although they said** **"must we fetch . . ." It was a miracle of the Lord. God provided** **water to meet the needs of the rebellious Israelites.**

Is it true that it doesn't matter how you worship, as long as you worship? Dogmatically, "***<u>Yes it does matter how a person worships</u>***." How we worship is of key importance . . . because one has to be keenly aware of Who or what is being worshiped. Is it God, self, or perhaps a mixture of both, or even an idol or philosophy? The trend in worship today, leans heavily toward entertainment as part of worship, and we justify this by saying Everyone needs that *feel good* experience, and we gotta keep trying until everyone is satisfied and happy—otherwise they may go to another church. It is obvious that people want entertainment, to make the Word of God more palatable. Too many churches have tailored their Sunday services to suite the tastes of its members. It is apparent we are bringing the world into the Church more and more, bit by bit, peace by peace, step by step. "For example, there is less and less emphasis on edifying the saints, and more and more stress on <u>entertaining</u> <u>unbelievers</u>." (The Truth War, by John MacArthur page 152)

I Timothy 1:3 warns against false teachers of the law. *"As I urged* *you when I went to Macedonia, stay there in Ephesus so that you* *may command certain men not to teach false doctrines any longer."* **II Peter 2:1** *"But there were also false prophets among the people,* *just as there will be false teachers among you. They will secretly* *introduce destructive heresies, even denying the sovereign Lord who* *bought them—bringing swift destruction on themselves."* **Jeremiah** **23:**1 *"Woe to the shepherds who are destroying and scattering the* *sheep of my pasture!" declares the LORD.*

Another point to look at these days: <u>Discipline</u> in churches seems to be falling by the wayside! Without discipline from the Word of God, there can be no proper directives! What is really needed in our worship is **inspiration,** *because* <u>*inspiration*</u> *leads to* <u>*motivation*</u> *and motivation leads to* <u>*action*</u>!!! This reaches one's heart and is much **more lasting** than the *feel good* experience. As in a *mountain top experience*, it is often present for the moment and gone with the next sunrise. Furnishing entertainment and amusements, in place of authentic worship, is destroying the modern day Church. There are three vitally important and necessary words which direct us to the Art of Worship. (1) the **Truth** of God's Word, (2) **Humility** before God, (3) **Receptivity** to the Holy Spirit. Then you are ready to honor the One key element in worship—**<u>*HOLY GOD*</u>**. This takes self-control, time, and discipline. Be humble enough to be receptive to the guidance of the Holy Spirit. Be ready to receive what God is saying. This is hardly possible with so much visiting and running around in the sanctuary before the worship service begins. We are in the House of the Lord, not a theater. When we come into the sanctuary for worship, it is time to focus on the Lord, Who is in His Holy temple. It is a great time for meditation and prayer.

<u>SEEKERS</u>

There is nothing amiss if one is an honest seeker: we need more seekers of this kind, asking **"What must I do to be saved?"** Paul and Silas were in jail, when a great earthquake opened the prison doors. The Jailer came running to see if the prisoners had escaped. He found Paul and Silas sitting there, and unharmed. They had no intention of escaping. What a powerful testimony. **Acts 16:30** *"And (the jailer) brought them (Paul and Silas) out, and said, Sirs, what must I do to be saved?"* KJV

Pastors long to hear individuals ask the question, "What must I do to be saved?" However, if someone actual were to ask this question, the pastor would probably be shocked, and perhaps even at a loss for what to say. It is seldom asked these days; probably because so many are under the false impression that they are saved already. Also, sad but true—so many are not concerned about how they may be saved. This is not their primary concern. It has to be recognized that in today's society we are so involved in multiple activities. We are not robots. Everyone, created in the image of God, has his or her peculiarities. People are seekers alright, but they are looking for the answers to this life, with its countless difficulties, in all the wrong places. Scientology has become very popular these days, as people are seeking for something <u>apart from the Church</u> to give meaning to their lives.

It is within the will of God that we are all different! It would be quite boring if we all looked the same and liked the same foods and entertainment. We don't always agree with one another. That is ok. We drive different cars. We like different sports, or perhaps we don't like sports at all because of what they have become. We go to different churches, all of which are various arms of the Lord's work on earth. We don't all like the sounds of rock; symphonic music; country music; jazz; opera; or what have you. As people go about their business, seeking happiness and meaning for their lives, we forget that we are really not of this world. This world is not our home! All of us are soon to leave this world. Therefore, we seldom stop to think about why we are here, and what we should do to be saved. This is what it means to be in the world. We are *free will agents,* to *pick and choose* what we want to believe and enjoy, especially when it comes to God: **at least we think we are** most of the time! However, John's Gospel reminds us—**15:19** *"If ye were of the world, the world would love his own: but because ye are not of the world, but I have chosen you out of the world, therefore the world hateth you."* KJV

It is not our mission in this life to have everyone love or like us. Popularity should not be our goal! We are to seek the Kingdom of God first, and above all else.

Is God going to accept our worship, if we continue to be confused as to how we are saved and enter into eternal life? Most people say "I believe in God," but haven't they read, or been told about **James 2:19** where it reads: *"You believe that there is one God. Good! Even the demons believe that—and shudder."* NIV

The devil and his demons will not be converted and be saved, because they will never give up their desire to be in control! They are not aware of the fact that they have already been defeated through the blood of Jesus! Hopefully our belief is not on the same par as that of the demons.

What must I do to be saved? <u>NOTHING!</u> God has already done all that is necessary for salvation. All the individual can do is to discipline self, and set aside time, from the daily routines of a week, for his or her needed rest in Christ. This rest and renewal will provide the incentive to receive God's free gift of eternal life, made possible through His Son Jesus. (**John 3-16**). There are multitudes of half-truths, but only one truth! *There is but one truth.* **John 14:6 *"Jesus saith unto him, I am the way, the truth, and the life: no man cometh unto the Father, but by me."***

Ephesians 4:4-6 *"There is one body, and one Spirit, even as ye are called in one hope of your calling; 5 One Lord, one faith, one baptism, 6 One God and Father of all, who is above all, and through all, and in you all.*

THE CHURCH BUILDING IS SACRED GROUND

Yes, the Church is indeed sacred ground, and must be treated as such, especially when we enter a church for the purpose of worship! If we could only learn, in a practical way, what it means to worship God in spirit and in truth. It is necessary that we first get ourselves out of the way: so to speak. It has been said, "We are our own worst enemy."

Psalm 100 reads: *"Shout for joy to the LORD, <u>all the earth</u>. 2 Worship the LORD with gladness; come before Him with joyful songs. 3 Know that the LORD is God. It is He who made us, and we*

are His; we are his people, the sheep of His pasture. **4** <u>*Enter his gates*</u> *with thanksgiving and His courts with praise; give thanks to Him and praise His name.* **5** *For the LORD is good and His love endures forever; His faithfulness continues through all generations."* NIV

Psalm 100 is a repetition of **Psalm 98**, sharing much of the same thought and content. Therefore, to openly cover our thoughts on this, please read the following King James Version of Psalm 98.

Psalm 98:1-9 *"O* <u>*sing unto the LORD*</u> <u>*a new song;*</u> *for he hath done marvelous things: his right hand, and his holy arm, hath gotten him the victory.* **2** *The LORD hath made known his salvation: his righteousness hath he openly shewed in the sight of the heathen.* **3** *He hath remembered his mercy and his truth toward the house of Israel: all the ends of the earth have seen the salvation of our God.* **4** <u>*Make a joyful noise*</u> *unto the LORD, all the earth:* <u>*make a loud noise,*</u> *and rejoice, and sing praise.* **5** *Sing unto the LORD with the harp;* <u>*with the harp,*</u> *and the voice of a psalm.* **6** *With* <u>*trumpets*</u> *and sound of* <u>*cornet*</u> *make a joyful noise before the LORD, the King.* **7** *Let the* <u>*sea roar,*</u> *and the fulness thereof; the world, and they that dwell therein.* **8** *Let the* <u>*floods clap their hands:*</u> *let* <u>*the hills be joyful*</u> *together* **9** *Before the LORD; for he cometh to judge the earth: with righteousness shall he judge the world, and the people with equity."* KJV

These Psalms give us much more to think about than at first thought! They instruct us to make a **joyful noise**, make a **loud noise, shout, worship with gladness,** and **sing joyful songs.** Does this mean that at corporate worship, we should, literally be following these directives? Hardly, as this would lead to pandemonium and more confusion would result. Especially, note here that there are directives given in these Psalms that speak about **all creation** *and* **let the sea roar** *and* **the earth** *and* **the floods clap their hands** *and* **let the hills be joyful together.** These cannot be part of a corporate worship experience. These Psalms are telling us that *all creation is to praise the Lord.*

The instruments mentioned in the Psalms, are to be used to glorify God. Many of the great composers wrote to the glory of God. In worship there is room for every instrument that God's grace has allowed Man to create, as long as the instruments are properly used to praise the Lord in the worship setting. The best example I know of is heard and seen in the music of The Mormon Tabernacle Choir (called America's Choir) and orchestra! What dedication, and a beautiful testimony this choir gives to their belief in Jesus Christ, as their personal Lord and Savior. Each member, of this fabulous body of Christians, is giving of their time, without pay, to praise Jesus Christ. Watch the faces of the choir members . . . they are not up front to call attention to themselves. A friend and member of the Tabernacle choir wrote me saying, "Singing in this choir is the least I can do for all my Savior has done for me."

Wesley's Bible explanation of **Psalm 98** gives us this bit of information: *"These Psalms are a call to praise the Lord as the righteous king. The whole world sings praises in anticipation of the righteousness that the Lord brings."*

These Psalms are really talking about our worship *inside* and *outside* the corporate worship setting. All of God's Creation is to worship and praise the Lord. So . . . let us all worship and honor the Lord, along with all of God's creation in our daily living! Let the world know where we stand! (**Psalm 98:9**) *"for he cometh to judge the earth: with righteousness shall he judge the world, and the people with equity."*

These Psalms direct us to go out into the world and praise God, along with the sea, the floods, the hills, etc! Let every day give joyful praise to the Lord, who owns and has created all: even more than we will ever see or understand. God gives to all His children every good and perfect gift. Let the world know you are a believer in the God of revelation, and that you have accepted His plan of salvation for your life, and all creation as well. **Romans 8:21-23** *". . . because the creation itself will be set free from its bondage to decay and obtain the glorious liberty of the children of God. 22 We know that the whole creation has been groaning in travail together until now; 23 and not only the creation, but we ourselves, who have the first fruits of the Spirit, groan inwardly as we wait for adoption as sons, the redemption of our bodies."*

Remember that God is present wherever two or three (or more) are gathered in His Name. Also . . . keep in mind that *"The Lord is in His Holy Temple . . . so let all the earth 'keep silence' before* **Him.**" There must be those moments in our worship, and in our life experiences, when we keep silent long enough to hear the voice of God! God is speaking, even if in the still small voice. **I Kings 19:12 "**. . . *And after the earthquake a fire; but the LORD was not in the fire: and after the fire a still small voice."*

We often want big shows, and demonstrations, but God says, "Listen! After all the tragic events in life (as in earthquakes, and fires), I am speaking in a still small voice." Are we still looking for vivid dramatizations to prove God's presence?

Corporate worship is a time to listen to God's voice speaking to us. This is a solemn period of shutting off the world around us, as we open ourselves to the presence of the Holy Spirit. This reminds me of the Temple United Methodist Church in the heart of downtown Chicago. As soon as you enter from the noisy streets of Chicago, and the door closes behind you, there is total silence. At worship we need to shut the door behind us, and in the sacred silence, hear the voice of God. This is the time set aside to honor God, and it is filled with great solemnity and joy, so be supremely happy when you are in the house of the Lord for corporate worship. No person, of any age, should ever think solemnity means there is a lack of joy. There is indeed a profoundly deep and lasting joy . . . not a passing emotion. However, a person has to experience this to know it! And we cannot hear and experience God's presence, when we are so busy trying to serve Him out of fear, and self pity, as was Elijah. (See 1 Kings 19 for the full account). He felt so alone, thinking he was the only faithful one left, and they were seeking his life.

In the daily life of the Christian, the world should be able to notice our witness to the God of all creation, and see in us something they also would like to have and experience for themselves. This witness should be as a **joyful shout within**: a testimony that God is in charge of your life and the lives of all Christians. It is so easy to sing "He's Got the Whole World in His Hands," but so difficult to live as though we truly believe it. There is a profound joy experienced in the quiet meditation of worship: of truly being still to know the God of Creation. Let your life be as a shout for joy, and as a witness to the lost, at home and around the world. We are to make known His Word each and every moment of every day, strong and certain as though we were shouting. Let the worship and praise of the Lord cover the whole earth. This is our witness.

THE HYMNS WE SING

A teenage boy told his friend that he was not going to church anymore, because it was so boring to sing those old, endless, and hard to understand hymns his grandparents enjoyed so much. Somewhere along the line of growing up, no one had explained why these hymns are so important to the Christian life. What we pastors have neglected to do, is to simply tell the congregation why a particular hymn was written. It is also a good practice to read aloud the words to a hymn once and in a while. This highlights the words, without concentrating the music. The music we love, and that has stood the test of time, means even more to us, when we know the story behind a particular hymn! A few examples of what I am referring to, are highlighted next:

WHY DID WILLAM SPAFFORD WRITE

It Is Well With My Soul?

"It Is Well With My Soul" is one of the most well-known hymns of our time. This hymn was written after two major traumas in the composer, Spafford's life. The first was the great Chicago Fire of

October 1871, which ruined him financially (he had been a wealthy businessman). The words of this hymn speak to the eternal hope all believers have, no matter what pain and grief befall them on earth.

In 1874, a French steam liner, the "Ville de Havre," was on its way back to France from America, with a large number of passengers. "On board the steamer was a Mrs. Spafford, with her four children. In mid-ocean a collision took place with a large sailing vessel, causing the steamer to sink in just half an hour. Nearly all on board were lost. Mrs. Spafford got her children out of their berths and up on the deck. On being told that the vessel would soon sink, she knelt down with her children in prayer, asking God that if possible they might be saved; or, be made willing to die, if that was His will. In a few minutes the vessel sank to the bottom of the sea, and the children were lost. One of the sailors found Mrs. Spafford floating in the water."

Mr. Spafford soon received a wire message from his wife in England, which simply read, "Saved alone." He immediately made the trip to England to pick up his wife and bring her back to the states. Standing on the deck of the ship heading across the Atlantic, Horatio Spafford soon saw with his own eyes the very spot where his four daughters and 226 other people drowned. Only because of his faith in God was he able to write, *"When sorrows like sea billows roll . . . it is well with my soul." (My Life And The Story Of The Gospel Hymns*, Sankey, 190)

THE WORDS TO "IT IS WELL WITH MY SOUL"

"When peace like a river, attendeth my way, when sorrows like sea-billows roll, what ever my lot, Thou hast taught me to say, "It is well, it is well with my soul."

Though Satan should buffet, though trials should come, let this blessed assurance control, that Christ hath regarded my helpless estate, and hath shed His own blood for my soul.

My sin, O, the bliss of this glorious thought! My sin not in part but the whole, is nailed to the cross and I bear it no more, praise the Lord, praise the Lord, O my soul!

And, Lord, haste the day when the faith shall be sight, thou clouds be rolled back as a scroll, the trump shall resound, and the Lord shall descend, 'Even so' it is well with my soul."

The lesson to be learned from this beautiful song is that no matter what happens to us in this life, no matter how great the pain and suffering, or the sorrows or joys, we need to heed the words of **Romans 8:28 *"God causes all things to work together for good to those who love Him."***

Look at it this way; either God is using His power to *teach* us something; or God is *allowing* something to happen—something that He could easily stop if He wanted to do so. **In any case, God is in control.** There are times when *bad things* happen to Christians and to everyone else. We don't become a Christian just to prevent these *bad things* from happening in our lives! Life does not become that *bed of roses* once we accept Christ as our Lord and Savoir! Neither do *all* bad things happen to us because of our personal sin. However, all *bad things* are present in our lives, because of the Adam's Fall. God allows what we consider to be 'bad' in our experiences, and we do not always have the ability to know why. The writer of Ecclesiastes records that some bad things happen *just because* (indeed, "*time and chance happen to us all")* according to **Ecclesiastes 9:11** *"I have seen something else under the sun: The race is not to the swift or the battle to the strong, nor does food come to the wise or wealth to the brilliant or favor to the learned; but time and chance happen to them all."* So when 'these things' happen to us, how should we respond? Will we blame God? Will we lose faith in God? Or, will we simply say, "It is well with my soul?"

WHAT IS AN EBENEZER?

Most people do not know the story behind the word Ebenezer, as found in the second stanza of the great hymn of the Christian Church *'Come Thou Fount of Every Blessing.'* The phrase that most people find difficult to understand is found in the second stanza: *'Hear I raise*

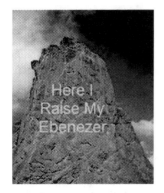

mine Ebenezer; hither by Thy help I'm come.' To help us come to a clearer understanding of the word Ebenezer we need to look at 1 **Samuel 4:1-11** and **5:1**. Ebenezer means "Stone of Help." It was the name of the memorial stone set up by Samuel to commemorate God's assistance to Israel in their great battle against the Philistines at Aphek. **(1 Samuel 7:7-12)** The Philistines had been defeated and the memorial stone is erected by Samuel. The spot where the stone was erected was somewhere "between Mizpeh and Shen," and it was called Ebenezer, because, "Thus far the Lord has helped us, or we have come this far with God's help." Samuel reminded the people of Israel that if they would but give up their idols, and turn their hearts to God, He would be their help. This they did, and the result was the destruction their enemies, the Philistines. To commemorate their victory over the Philistines, Samuel erected this monument of stone.

Literally speaking, an Ebenezer is a *stone of help* . . . a reminder of God's real Holy Presence and Divine aid. For Christians, an Ebenezer can be anything that reminds us of God's presence and help: the Bible, the Holy Communion, the Cross, a picture, a fellow believer, a hymn, i.e., anything that serves as a reminder of God's love, presence and help in our lives. These are our "Ebenezers."

Speaking of "Ebenezer," found in the hymn *'Come Thou Fount of Many Blessings'* Gary Parrett, Professor of Educational Ministries and Worship, at Gordon-Conwell, a non-denominational theological seminary in Boston, Massachusetts, has written a thought provoking article for the *Christianity Today* magazine, called "**Raising Ebenezer**," in which he argues **for preserving** archaic language in Christian hymns **_because they inform our faith in ways that contemporary language cannot._** "Here I raise my Ebenezer" is a strong statement, that in God I find my blessings and strength, and here **in God, I take my stand**. God is the Rock of my salvation . . . there is none else!

We should give thanks to God for the wonderful Ebenezers He has given us in this life. May each and every one of us always be blessed by the grace and peace of Jesus Christ through the Ebenezers (help) God has placed in our lives! This is where we take our stand: God does help us! Martin Luther took his stand (Ebenezer) during the Reformation, knowing he was within the will of God, according to Scripture. God helps us all the time: in stormy weather and in the sunshine moments of our lives!

Yes . . . Americans, and all peoples of earth, are told, as were the children of Israel, to give up their idols and turn their hearts to God. Then He will be our help . . . our Ebenezer! Jesus is our stone of help: On Christ the Solid Rock I Stand, taken from the Hymn "My Hope is Built."

Verse
My hope is built on nothing less
Than Jesus' blood and righteousness.
I dare not trust the sweetest frame,
But wholly trust in Jesus' Name.
Refrain
On Christ the solid Rock I stand,
All other ground is sinking sand;
All other ground is sinking sand.

2 Chronicles 7:14 *"If my people which are called by My name, shall humble themselves, and pray, and seek My face, and turn from* *their wicked ways, then will I hear from heaven, and will forgive their sin, and will heal their land."* KJV

THE STORY BEHIND "AMAZING GRACE"

Amazing grace was written by John Newton, and has become one of the most beloved hymns of all time: indeed the staple in the hymnals of many denominations. John spoke of himself as a professional sinner who was lost. The story does not end here however: because John (as he puts it) was found by Jesus.

John Newton was born in London on July 24, 1725, the son of a commander of a merchant ship which sailed the Mediterranean. At the early age of 11, John went to sea with his father and made 6 sea voyages with his father before his father's retirement. In 1744 John was working aboard the Man-of-War, the H. M. S. Harwich. Finding conditions on board intolerable, he deserted, but was soon recaptured and publicly flogged and demoted from midshipman to common seaman.

At the age of 22, John, a wretched sinner, was converted from being a daring blasphemer against God, into a devout believer in Christ. He wrote: "But let me not fail to praise that grace which could pardon, that blood which could expiate, such sins as mine. Yea, the Ethiopian may change his skin and the leopard his spots. I, who was the willing slave of every evil, possessed with a legion of unclean spirits, have been spared and saved, and changed, to stand as a monument of His almighty power for ever." (Out of the Depths, by John Newton . . . P.47)

Although he had had some early religious instruction from his mother, who had died when he was a child, he had long since given up any religious convictions. However, on a homeward voyage, while he was attempting to steer the ship through a violent storm, he experienced what he was to refer to later, as his "great deliverance." He recorded in his journal that when all seemed lost and the ship would surely sink, he cried out: "Lord, have mercy upon us." Later in his cabin he reflected on what he had said and began to believe that God had brought him through the storm and that grace had begun to work for him.

For the rest of his life, he observed the anniversary of May 10, 1748 as the day of his conversion: a day of humiliation in which he subjected his will to a *higher power*. "Through' many dangers, toils and snares, I have already come; 'tis grace has brought me safe thus far, and grace will lead me home." He continued in the slave trade for a time after his conversion; however, he saw to it that the slaves under his care were treated humanely.

In 1750 John Newton married Mary Catlett, with whom he had been in love for many years. By 1755, after a serious illness, he had given up seafaring forever. During his days as a sailor he had begun to educate himself, teaching himself Latin, among other subjects. From 1755 to 1760 Newton was a surveyor of the tides at Liverpool, where he came to know George Whitefield, deacon in the Church of England: evangelistic preacher, and leader of the Calvinistic Methodist Church. Newton became Whitefield's enthusiastic disciple. During this period Newton also met and came to admire John Wesley, called the founder of Methodism. Newton's self-education continued, and he learned Greek and Hebrew. What determination: **what Goal setting, lest he fall short of his calling**.

He decided to become a minister and applied to the Archbishop of York for ordination. The Archbishop refused his request, but Newton persisted in his goal, and he was subsequently ordained by the Bishop of Lincoln, and accepted the curacy of Olney, Buckinghamshire. Newton's church became so crowded during services that it had to be enlarged. He preached not only in Olney, but in other parts of the country. In 1767 the poet William Cowper settled at Olney, and he and Newton became friends.

Cowper helped Newton with his religious services, and on his tours to other places. They not only held a regular weekly church service, but also began a series of weekly prayer meetings, for which their goal was to write a new hymn for each one. Among Newton's contributions, which are still loved and sung today, are: *'How Sweet the Name of Jesus Sounds'* and *'Glorious Things of Thee Are Spoken,'* as well as *'Amazing Grace.'*

When we take time to read the words of most of the great hymns, without singing them, a sharper image of the meaning of the words comes into focus. It is very interesting to take note that, Amazing Grace is the only hymn that can be played in its entirety on the black notes of the piano. Remember, Newton had been a black slave trader.

WORDS TO AMAZING GRACE

Amazing grace! how sweet the sound
That saved a wretch like me!
I once was lost, but now am found,
Was blind, but now I see.
'Twas grace that taught my heart to fear,
And grace my fears relieved;
How precious did that grace appear,
The hour I first believed!
Through many dangers, toils and snares,
I have already come;
'Tis grace has brought me safe thus far,
And grace will lead me home.
The Lord has promised good to me,
His word my hope secures;
He will my shield and portion be,
As long as life endures.
Yes, when this flesh and heart shall fail,
And mortal life shall cease;
I shall possess, within the veil,
A life of joy and peace.
The earth shall soon dissolve like snow,
The sun forbear to shine;

But God, who called me here below,
Will be forever mine.
When we been there ten thousand years
bright shining as the sun,
We've no less days to sing God's praise
then when we'd first begun.

Newton was not only a prolific hymn writer, but also kept extensive journals and wrote many letters. Historians accredit his journals and letters for much of what is known today about the eighteenth century slave trade. In Cardiphonia, or the Utterance of the Heart (a series of devotional letters), he aligned himself with the Evangelical revival, reflecting the sentiments of his friend John Wesley and Methodism.

Newton drew large congregations and influenced many: among them was William Wilberforce, who would one day become a leader in the campaign for the abolition of slavery. Newton continued to preach until the last year of his life, although he was blind by that time. He died in London on December 21, 1807. Infidel and libertine turned minister in the Church of England, he was secure in his faith that amazing grace would lead him home. This reminds me of the conversion of Saul, who became known as Paul. By the grace of God people can and do change.

What we see at this point is the fact that many new hymns (at that time) were being written, most of them growing out of the writer's having overcome tragedy and sin in life. They were not written for profit, but to glorify God alone. The intent was to lead others, who had similar experiences, to confess their sin and turn to Jesus. **II Corinthians 1:3,4** *"Blessed be God, even the Father of our Lord Jesus Christ, the Father of mercies, and the God of all comfort; 4 Who comforteth us in all our tribulation, that we may be able to comfort them which are in any trouble, by the comfort wherewith we ourselves are comforted of God."*

We need to be led by that same Spirit, and by others who have walked ahead of us to guide our course: who have, figuratively speaking, walked in our steps.

Contemporary music is not all bad! Two outstanding samples of contemporary inspirational music come to mind: *"Come to Jesus"* and *"People Need the Lord."* Others have made it into the hymnal: *"Hymn of Promise"* written in 1986, and *"Lord of the Dance."* written in 1967. Also there is countless inspirational contemporary music being written today by sincere Christian persons!

TIMES ARE CHANGING, WE DON'T

What is happening to music today? We have all heard that times are changing, and they are! But, such a shallow conclusion does not answer the question. The question we should seek to answer simply and honestly is this: Are things getting better, worse, or more complicated and confusing? We can agree that Man has gotten himself into an unsolvable situation. Is it difficult to have a happy life when things around you are deteriorating so rapidly? Frustration can cause despair and loss of hope. Will the storm clouds ever give way to sunshine, happiness and security. Much of the world is being engulfed in the rising river of degenerate filth. With the abandonment of virtue, righteousness and personal integrity, traditional marriage, and family life . . . we have created what appears to be an insurmountable problem. Yet in spite of Man's fallen condition, the world is still beautiful, filled with many good and sincere people. God has provided a way to live in this world, and yet not be contaminated by it. **Romans 12:21** records: ***"Do not be overcome of evil, but <u>overcome evil with good.</u>"***

In these *changing times*, many colleges and universities no longer have an organ program in their curriculum. This is not a good thing for the individual who wants to take up organ proficiency! What if you wanted to be a coach in a fine school, only to discover that program no longer exists? What a silly statement! We are living in a world that has become preoccupied with television, sports, greed, filthy language, and sex. This is where the money is to be made! **Isaiah 53:6** sums it up very well. *"We all, like sheep, have gone astray, each of us has turned to his own way; and the LORD has laid on him the iniquity of us all."*

As someone has said: *"Your ego is writing checks your body cannot cash."* That is to say that we have spread ourselves much too thin. Egotistically, we make dogmatic decisions, but later find we an unable to follow them up. This reminds me of the average New Years resolution, which last about a week if one is fortunate.

In the midst of God's blessings, we find ourselves being consumed with all the possible activities with which mankind can be involved, and left with little enthusiasm to pursue proper goals. Think about this—What did people do before: stereo; television, cell phones, texting, computers, recorders, I Pods, and the other endless chain of new items coming up almost daily? We would be at a loss for something to do if we didn't have television, sports of all kinds, rock and roll, rap, Hollywood's obsession with films depicting drugs, explicit sex, filthy language, and cursing; which is blaspheming the Holy Name of God and that of His Son Jesus Christ. Television's Comedy Central is amongst the worst offenders: although this show has an endless amount of competition when it comes to cursing, and the use filthy language to communicate. This kind of entertainment (if you can call it that) brings thoughts and attitudes to mind that are contrary to the Word and Will of God. It destroys inspiration, and leads to self destruction. In today's world there is little time to fulfill goals (that may have been made with good intention at one time) and now, later on, the situation has changed, and the plans once made have fallen apart. Now, unable to become involved in the arts for a better life, lesser values emerge.

We are living in **one world**, that is to say, what happens in Europe, the Middle East, China, India, Pakistan, etc., has an affect upon those living in the United States. There are many who spend their time doing 'what comes naturally' or 'following the paths of least resistance.' It is almost impossible to set goals and stick to them, because we are sidetracked by the world's obsession with things. We are addicted to selfish and fleshly desires!

Of course we still have fine music and composes who give us meaningful and inspirational music. These individuals are persons **who have set and kept their goals,** even if their motivation were for profit. They rejected lesser availabilities, and are determined **never to give in** to the paths of least resistance, which would cause them to forsake their hopes and dreams. We are a people of complainers, and we are a dissatisfied people, without the vaguest idea as to why this is the case. The answer is simple: God is simply not a part of the majority's plan for this life. Are people to busy for God? Is God too busy for us?

Pause now, and think about **Isaiah 5:20 "Woe to those who call evil good and good evil, who put darkness for light and light for darkness, who put bitter for sweet and sweet for bitter."** NIV

Is it too strong a statement to say these words apply to our time under the Son (I didn't mean sun)? Judgment day is coming, and Jesus is going to return, as He promised He would, but within God's time table! **2 Peter, chapter 3:8-11.** *"But do not forget this one thing, dear friends: With the Lord a day is like a thousand years, and a thousand years are like a day.* **9** *The Lord is not slow in keeping his promise, as some understand slowness. He is patient with you, not wanting anyone to perish, but everyone to come to repentance.* **10** *But the day of the Lord will come like a thief. The heavens will disappear with a roar; the elements will be destroyed by fire, and the earth and everything in it will be laid bare.* **11** *Since everything will be destroyed in this way, what kind of people ought you to be? You ought to live holy and godly lives."* NIV

ALL IS NOT WELL

Maxie Dunnam asks an extremely important question in his book "The Grace-Filled Life", (Used by permission) *"Is there a nation more blessed than we? The normal blessings God has bestowed upon us are beyond number. Yet we continue to ravage our environment*

in destructive ways. No less than 30 million people are living in poverty. The unemployment rate is nearing 10%. We have a drug culture that could lead to our demise. Racisms still eats at the soul of our country. We are presently fighting wars in Afghanistan, and Iraq, and another is threatened in Iran. The sword of Damocles hangs over our head in the form of a raging national neurotic insecurity."

Activities are going on in our midst that we feel just cannot be happening. But, just because we are not part of this action, nor do we see it in our back yard, it is difficult to believe these kinds of activities are really taking place!

The events in our cities, and even small towns, would make one think: "Woops, we are back at the foot of Mt. Sinai again." (See Mt. Sinai Section, page 9) Sex bars are common, and so called adult establishments are all around us. There are 27 casinos (as of June 1211) in Iowa, and this number is growing, not to mention other states and locations. Do we need to say more . . . just watch the news! **We need to get back to the truth!** And just because I am a *good person*, and live in a respectable neighborhood, doesn't mean all is well! And it should be added at this point *being good does not mean you are saved!* There is only One Who is 'good' and that is God. **Matthew 19:17 *"Why do you ask me about what is good ?" Jesus replied. "There is only One who is good. If you want to enter life, obey the commandments."*** NIV

Surely the human being, <u>**created in the image of God**</u>, should be able to choose music that is uplifting, and has lasting beauty. Secular music should at least have a tune that people could actually whistle, hum, or sing, regardless of a person's age. It is apparent that the world is not interested in quality music at this time, as is evidenced in a recent observation of an entertainer at Rockefeller Plaza, on *The Good Morning America* Show. A very popular and famous entertainer of this generation was performing. I had never heard of him before this showing. I don't even remember his name! He was literally bouncing up and down off and on the piano stool, upon which he was <u>almost</u> seated, as he attempted to play the piano and sing with a mike at his lips: along with the loud accompaniment of the guitars, drums and others who were trying to perform with him. The audience went **_wild_** waiving their arms and shouting in such a manner that the Lord's Second coming could not have received a greater ovation. (When seeing this sort of behavior at worship it a sad commentary on how far we have fallen from the true worship of God.) However, this is just a very small grain of the sand when compared to the endless groups popping up all over the world, to play their peculiar sounds: many of whom are decked out with painted faces, tattoos, and tattered clothing, while jumping around as though they all had ants in their pants. Hey . . . I am just telling it like it is!

Subtle satan has taken over the minds of many young and very impressionable individuals, along with younger parents as well. Why are these *neurotic sounds* so captivating? It is very evident that today's performers are extremely talented. The problem is—they have not directed their talents toward better, and more lasting, relaxing, meaningful, constructive and inspiring music. Going back to what has been stated earlier, we can all relate to these sounds because anyone can sing as well, and even better, than most entertainers of this generation, *although* we cannot play their instruments . . . but we try to imitate them none-the-less.

THERE SHALL ALWAYS BE MUSIC IN THE WORLD

There shall always be music in our world. But, there is only one music with which to praise God, and this is music that comes out of the faith-filled heart that God has touched: a heart that is not concerned about financial gain. Faith comes from hearing the Word of God. In **Romans 10:17** *"__Faith comes from hearing__ the message, and the message is heard through the Word of Christ."*

When Isaiah walked into the temple of the Lord, he heard music that was so glorious, or as he put it . . . "The singing of the heavenly choir was so profoundly beautiful, glorious, and unworldly, the very Temple shook to its foundations." Music reaches the foundation of our souls.

The words to praise songs, (the ever-growing way many seek to worship God), in too many instances, come from the pen of persons (young and inexperienced) who are seeking to gain fame by writing new contemporary material. Go to the back of any Christian book store and see the endless albums put out by contemporary composers. Admittedly, there are some great and inspirational albums. The great hymns of the church, for the most part, are no longer there. There are seemingly endless recordings of contemporary and gospel music. This is acceptable as long as such music grows out of the Biblical message, and is humble in its demeanor. However, there is still a great need for hymns of the Christian tradition.

<u>WHAT'S GOING ON?</u>

Please understand that I am not pointing a finger at contemporary or traditional worship: **much is lacking in both**. Therefore, this material is not written to be critical of the way persons worship at a contemporary service or at a traditional worship service. We have enough divisions in our midst already! This material is written to direct our thoughts toward **Biblical Worship;** thus hopefully to put an end to our being divided in the way we worship. Our communities need to see the church as truly a united congregation, that worships the same Lord together. As of now, many churches are a divided congregation: two churches using the same building. Where do we take our stand as we witness to persons in the community? Churches are proud to boast of having contemporary and traditional services. We think we are meeting the needs of people with two services. No church, or any other facility, can please everyone within our diverse population. Even God sent His son that we might be saved . . . He is the One Way. God did not send two or three saviors, because He was trying to meet the various needs of his people, and give the appearance that there are several different ways to be saved. Jesus alone is the Way. Biblical worship, in essence, is asking us to align the way we worship with what is in the Bible. (See Biblical Worship, page 25)

Recently I was browsing through a large pamphlet of a church with which I am very familiar. There is an eye opening photo near the end of this material. It was a picture of the year 1925 Men's Bible Class of that church. I tried to count these men, but they are not standing in exact rows, which made it almost impossible to get an accurate count, but there were at least 110 men dressed in suit and tie in that Bible class. Where have all our men gone? Today's population is much larger! Our churches should be filled to capacity! It is not the answer to cast this question aside saying, "Times have changed." This is much too often used as a copout. It is our environment and methods that have changed! People have always been sinners, but today we are equipped with new technology. People use these new abilities, offered through technology, to accomplish the same old selfish goals. Technology has made it possible to view or hear anything. It is the window to the eye-gate and ear-gate that has changed. And we are too weak to shut the blinds and take care of what really matters in life. Churches are strong where men take the leadership roll. Homes are on a solid foundation where respected husbands and fathers lead. satan has placed so many distractions before us. It is time we get our ducks in a row, as they say, and prioritize our lives. Nothing is more important than getting straight with God, and knowing God.

Bible Study groups are one possible answer to understanding God's plan for us. But which Bible version or paraphrase should we use? Personally, I prefer the King James Version of the Bible, because of its poetic format. Many today feel this version is outdated: which is absolutely ridiculous. But it is not as easily understood as the newer versions and paraphrases. Nevertheless, I would recommend the King James Version as the *foundation version*: the version to use for Scripture memorization because of its poetic form. I use the King

James Version, but often use other translations and paraphrases as one could use a commentary. It is always helpful to see how others have translated passages we find difficult in the poetic King James Version. At this point (laying memorization aside for a moment) I really like the New International Version of the Bible, for Bible study classes, and for pew Bibles. On your computer, type into your browser the following site—(biblegaterway.com). You will be amazed what you have found.

TRADITION

In Maxie Dunnam's book **"The Grace-Filled Life" page 64,** he makes a very profound and thought provoking statement. Speaking of tradition he writes: *"We know that traditions, rules, and laws are essential, giving us a necessary sense of order, structure, and continuity. Without them we could be like leaves <u>blowing aimlessly</u> in a wind."*

These words bring to mind what is written in **Ephesians 4:4-14** *"There is one body and one Spirit, just as you were called in one hope of your calling; 5 one Lord, one faith, one baptism; 6 one God and Father of all, who is above all, and through all, and in you all. 7 But to each one of us grace was given according to the measure of Christ's gift. 8 Therefore He says: "When He ascended on high, He led captivity captive, And gave gifts to men." 9 (Now this, "He ascended"—what does it mean but that He also first descended into the lower parts of the earth? 10 He who descended is also the One who ascended far above all the heavens, that He might fill all things.) 11 And He Himself gave some to be apostles, some prophets, some evangelists, and some pastors and teachers, 12 for the equipping of the saints for the work of ministry, for the edifying of the body of Christ, 13 till we all come to the unity of the faith and of the knowledge of the Son of God, to a perfect man, to the measure of the stature of the fullness of Christ; 14 that we should no longer be children, <u>tossed to</u>*

and fro and carried about with every wind of doctrine, by the trickery of men, in the cunning craftiness of deceitful plotting."

Without tradition, we will lose much that is valuable to our past, present and future. When our two sons were growing up, during the Christmas season, we had the traditional manger scene displayed in our living room. I had constructed it out of old orange crates. The characters and animals used were purchased at the local dime store. Our boys always enjoyed moving the camels closer to the manger scene as Christmas drew nearer. Sometimes we would find a camel standing on the roof of the manger scene. On Christmas morning our boys would place the baby Jesus figure into the manger inside the old barn, where also stood a cow looking out of the window. They have never forgotten this little but meaningful tradition. We all have traditions in our lives. Living without tradition is almost like living with no law to guide us. Where there is no law the people perish. **Proverbs 29:18** *"Where there is no vision* (i.e. the word of God)*, the people perish: but he that keepeth the law, happy is he."* KJV The law is the Word of God. Without Him, we perish!

THE PROBLEMS
IN THE FIFTY'S THROUGH TODAY

sATAN HAS hIS HAND IN OUR AFFAIRS AT ALL TIMES! hE KNOWS hIS TIME IS SHORT!!! hE IS ALAWYS ON THE ATTACK. hE KNOWS THAT IF hE IS GOING TO DEFEAT CHRISTIANITY, hE MUST DO IT THROUGH PEOPLE. hE ALSO KNOWS THAT IF THE LORD'S DAY IS DEFEATED, CHRISTIANITY WILL BE DEALT A DEADENING BLOW. ARE WE UNWITTINLY DEFEATING THE LORD'S DAY IN THE WAY WE WORSHIP, OR IN THE WAY WE DON'T WORSHIP? YOU SEE, sATAN, I.E., THE dEVIL, DOES NOT *KNOW, OR DOES NOT WANT TO RECOGNIZE*

THE FACT THAT hE (satan, the old devil) IS ALREADY DEFEATED BECAUSE OF THE ATONING BLOOD OF JESUS!

How we worship is the distinctive dividing line between those who really know God, and those who just *think* they know God. There is a difference! All human selfish interests must be dethroned, in order that Christ may sit upon the throne of our lives. What is it that inspires people when gathered as a congregation for worship? It is most helpful to look at **John, chapter 9**. When Jesus was working miracles during His earthly ministry. The people did not know Who Jesus was at that time. In the light of these words (John 9), ask yourself the question "Do I really know Jesus any more than those in chapter 9 of John" They had all sorts of conclusions as to how Jesus could do miracles: the silliest of all was their conclusion that Jesus was a sinner.

HOW THE FATHER OF LIES GETS HOLD OF US

Satan or the devil (whatever you call him) is the **father of lies.** he knows exactly how to get the upper hand with the youth and adults of any age.

Most any teenager on a date can sing to his gal as good as Elvis. However, Elvis, was very handsome, and had a magnetic sex appeal as a young man, and was being *"promoted"* by anyone who could make their fortunes through him. We all know, along with Hollywood, that sex, filthy language, cursing, and religion sell at the box office. Hear a common sound with fitting background music often enough, and somehow we fallen creatures begin to enjoy it, especially when nothing else of better quality is being offered. In other words, tragically, we can and do relate to that which is based upon satan's lies. When told a lie often enough, a person soon believes it! So today the philosophy is—*Everyone is doing it, so . . . almost anything goes.* If satan's lies can't get a person hooked right away, that is fine . . . satan is patient.

Silly, thoughtless, and meaningless phrases are so contagious. Example: in the modern and current vernacular, events and people must be *'real cool.'* You are *in* if you use clichés like this. I like to remind people that if it is **cool,** that means—**it's not so hot.** We really enjoy using those tripe, stereotyped meaningless expressions, and yet we complain if a Spanish speaking person waits on us at our favorite restaurant, because we can't quite understand him. We say "If they are going to live here, let them learn our language." I would suggest we haven't learned to use English properly ourselves. I am told that English is one of the most difficult languages to learn because of all the popular twists and phrases we have added to it. "Go jump in the lake, or go fly a kite" . . . is that what we really mean?

It seems that most movies and television programs have made it a habit to use the expression **"Oh My God."** Relatively speaking, as compared to the other endless forms of expression used by the media: you may think this isn't so bad. I like to ask persons who use this "O My God" phrase—"Just who is your God?" Persons today are using the name of God so flippantly! It is wrong! In the early history of the Israelites, it was felt that the name for God should never be audibly spoken . . . God's Name was too holy to speak aloud! Using God's Name in this manner is like habitually swearing. If the person, actor, producer, or script writers really knew God, they could never use His name in such a casual and inappropriate manner. Apparently, when heard often enough, our speech becomes common and acceptable! We so easily follow the paths of whatever everyone else is doing or saying: the paths of least resistance. We want to be popular and *in!*

DETERIORATING EVEN MORE

Today, all one has to do is gather together some sounds/noise with a beat that people can rap to, and you have a hit. We were in Sioux City at a Pizza Palace, when someone put a coin in the juke box. Suddenly, all we heard was *"boom, boom, boom,"* and this noise didn't stop. We told the waitress something had gone wrong with the juke box: we thought it needed to be unplugged, to prevent further damage to the instrument. She quickly replied, "Oh no, that is our latest recording." The jukebox is ok.

When it comes to music used for worship, there are many people who have what is termed as 'a tin ear.' There are multitudes out there, who cannot sing or play an instrument properly, because they cannot hear the right pitch. Some of these individuals have an insensitivity to melodic, rhythmic, and harmony variety in music. Jack Benny's daughter Joan, tells how her father always had the problem with hearing the right pitch when playing his violin. He wasn't quite sure when he had it right. The result was that Jack, and many others like him, would be a bit flat or sharp when trying to hit a particular note. This is why, as a comedian, Jack got many a laugh from the audience, when he purposefully played his violin so badly; even though he was quite good when playing for benefits. However, if a person does not have the inability to hear pitches on target, or be right on pitch, this does not mean the individual cannot enjoy and have appreciation for great and inspirational music. Jack loved, and was very familiar with the classics. Of course these individuals can learn to like any of the music that is out there. Most everyone has talents of one form or another. **Ephesians 4:11-13** *"It was he who gave some to be apostles, some to be prophets, some to be evangelists, and some to be pastors and teachers,* **12** *to prepare God's people for works of service, so that the body of Christ may be built up* **13** *until we all reach unity in the faith and in the knowledge of the Son of God and become mature, attaining to the whole measure of the fullness of Christ."*

Pastors and seminaries should know that the worship of the Lord must be lovingly guarded against the heresy of seeking popularity by flowing with the tide. God cannot be worshiped by combining the sounds of the non-believing or heathen parts of world, with church music by adding religious words. Oil and water do not mix. If you feel that worship is boring, and often it is to people of all ages, then let us remember we are all still under construction. The Church is to be in the world, but not of the world. If worship is boring, examine your life: recognize the presence of God in worship. If the Church would only stand for something, and stop trying to be all things to all people: it would be an honor to be in the Church. It must be noted right off the top . . . our pastors, denominations, and seminaries are going to be held accountable for what they are teaching, when it comes to the worship God, and how to conduct a worship service that is acceptable to the Lord. Pastors and seminary instructors are challenged, as never before in these modern times, to know how to worship God without compromising **Biblical Worship**. The Word of God in the Bible does not change. Right and wrong does not change with the tide. Truth does not change . . . but we have badly bent the truth to suit our will and pleasure! **Hebrews 13:8** *"Jesus Christ the same yesterday, and to day, and forever."*

Hebrews 4:14 " *. . . be no more children, tossed to and for and carried about with every wind of doctrine, by the sleight of men, and cunning craftiness, whereby they lie in wait to deceive."*

HOLLYWOOD IN sATAN'S PLAN

Watching a movie in a theater is quite an experience. Usually the music is unreasonably loud, yet much of the spoken word is not loud enough to understand what is being said. Hollywood has forgotten how to make movies, and this is tragic, because **movies teach, and inspire behavior**. The movies of today are telling the younger generation (including parents) how to talk and act. The lesson learned at the movies is simple: to be macho a person needs to curse and use as many filthy words as possible in a given sentence. This is an unacceptable way to communicate! Movies do a great job of brainwashing. Having been brainwashed, such inappropriate use of the English language soon shows up as part of our every day conversation for small children, young people, teenagers and adults. People want to be macho. The fact is filmmakers are **not** macho, but they are very **childish**.

Years ago in a movie staring Bob Hope and Bing Crosby, there was a scene depicting the Universal Studio logo (a mountain with a circle of stars circling it). Bob says, as they looked at the Universal logo "Movies are your best entertainment." Not true any more! It doesn't add anything to the movie or its story line to insert swearing, and sex scenes. Many films have a great message, but the story is cluttered with the inappropriate use of words and quite explicit sexual activities. In director Ron Howard's film "Cocoon," instead of using the phrase "God be with you," they say "May the force be with you." Such subtlety is used countless times in movies making.

Today's Hollywood films are satan's greatest educational tool. We are taught how to act, speak, kill, how to commit adultery, and unspeakably more. It is really evident that screen writers and producers are doing their very best to use as many filthy (unspeakable) words, as possible in a given sentence. Years ago we never heard of rating motion pictures. The Roman Catholic Church did sensor what movies their members could watch. There is no way to know if this was honored by Catholics.

Hollywood wanted to get rid of censorship, so they came up with a rating system of their own: *G*—General Audiences, *PG*—Parental Guidance, as some material may not be suitable for children; *PG-13*—Parents Strongly Cautioned . . . some material may be inappropriate for children under 13; *R*—Restricted . . . children under 17 require an accompanying parent or adult guardian <u>sometimes</u>; At least half the films shown on television are R rated, and anyone can turn on television and watch these regardless of their age. *NC-17*—No one 17 and under admitted; *X* rated movies informing people that this movie has explicit sex scenes for ages 18 and older; *XXX* movies are shown in triple X theaters, and in porn shops, and again a person has to be 18 years of age or older. In our depravity, who wants to pay good money to watch a G-rated film?

I have often wondered, why age 18 should mean that an individual is an adult. As I recall, 18 is a very indeterminate age. These young people are at the point of making important decisions about their lives, and there are multitudes of unanswered questions. Sorry—Age 18 does not automatically turn a person into an adult! People are not all going to be adult because they are 18 years of age. When does a person really become an adult, and what is the definition of adult anyway? Hollywood thinks they know. To most filmmakers being an adult means that you can watch and listen to anything they put on the screens of the world, if you are 18 years of age and older. This is pathetic! This doesn't make sense. Well, everyone reading this knows what I mean. Of course the governments of the world agree as well.

Violence is also the order of the day in motion pictures. Let action take the place of an inspiring story line. It appears that movie makers just want to show off their newest computerized techniques.

Hollywood tells us they are depicting *"the real world."* If this is true, then we all ought to get on our knees and pray for forgiveness, for being the 'animals' we have become. Hollywood has forgotten that we are **not animals**, but **God's best Creation**; we are even created <u>in the image of God</u>.

It's all about money—the bottom line! If your child has not heard a filthy word or cursing in the home, he will hear and see these abominations in the theater and on television! The whole matter is beyond belief and out of control! Hollywood and the movie makers in the main, are selling their souls to satan through the production of such material, and their reason for doing so is simply—profit and fame. And when we pay to see such trash, we are supporting satan's plan. The true 'adult' does not use such language! Such use of words is actually childish. **1 Corinthians 13:11** *"When I was a child, I spake as a child, I understood as a child, I thought as a child: but when I became a man, I put away childish things."* KJV

Matthew 18:6 *"But whoso shall <u>offend</u> one of these little ones which believe in me, it were better for him that a millstone were hanged about his neck, and that he were drowned in the depth of the sea."*

Many adults, in other words, have not learned how to use proper English, so they make up for it with all sorts of what many consider to be *macho* idiosyncrasies. Remember what has already been written in this material . . . we become what we are exposed to over and over again, regardless of our age. We are all under construction! The sad truth is that many of the stories being told in movies are really fine, and inspirational: but, the entertainment and inspirational values are lost as soon as God's name is taken in vain, and filthy language is added along with at least one sex scene. A relative of mine has written a novel based on a true story; but, the publisher told her she needed to add some swearing, and some filthy words in order for her book to sell. This is a sad commentary, but nothing new!

The Bible tells us there is only one unforgivable sin, and that is blasphemy against the Holy Spirit. Judgment day is coming Hollywood! **Mark 3:29** *"Whoever blasphemes against the Holy Spirit will never be forgiven; he is guilty of an eternal unpardonable sin."*

HUMANS ARE INCURABLY RELIGIOUS HUMANS MUST WORSHIP SOMETHING OR SOMEONE!

People all over the world look at creation and have this inbred sense that what they see in the world inspires some sort of worship toward something or someone. The sun, the moon, the stars . . . well whatever . . . have been the object of worship. The truth is that people are incurably religious! By the grace of God, there is an inbred sense, that there are powers in the world beyond ourselves. **Romans 1:19,20** *"Because that which may be known of God is manifest in them; for God hath shewed it unto them. 20 For the invisible things of him* *from the creation of the world are clearly seen, being understood by the things that are made, even his eternal power and Godhead; so that they are without excuse."* KJV

Listen to what Paul ran into in Athens: **Acts 17:22-31** *"Paul then stood up in the meeting of the Areopagus and said: "Men of Athens! I see that in every way you are very religious. 23 For as I walked around and looked carefully at your objects of worship, I even found an altar with this inscription: TO AN UNKNOWN GOD. Now what you worship as something unknown I am going to proclaim to you. 24 "The God who made the world and everything in it is the Lord of heaven and earth and does not live in temples built by hands. 25 And he is not served by human hands, as if he needed anything, because he himself gives all men life and breath and everything else. 26 From one man he made every nation of men, that they should inhabit the whole earth; and he determined the times set for them and the exact places where they should live. 27 God did this so that men would seek him and perhaps reach out for him and find him, though he is not far from each one of us. 28 'For in him we live and move and have our being.' As some of your own poets have said, 'We are his offspring.' 29 "Therefore since we are God's offspring, we should not think that the divine being is like gold or silver or stone—an image made by man's design and skill. 30 In the past God overlooked such ignorance, but now he commands all people everywhere to repent. 31 For he has set a day when he will judge the world with justice by the man he has appointed. He has given proof of this to all men by raising him from the dead."* NIV

The Apostle Paul was quite surprised in Athens when he noticed an altar dedicated to an unknown god . . . **just in case they missed one**. The *truth* is . . . Jesus Christ is our only hope for eternal life! How thankful we should be that Christianity is **born of God, and not from the philosophies of Man.** It is from the philosophies of Man that religions are born.

Think of the weekly gatherings at our prestigious colleges, where hundreds of thousands gather to observe a ceremony where men dressed in strange garb are acting out a violent drama of conquest. Fans of professional football are probably not even aware that their behavior <u>could</u> *be* described as worship! These fans pay more than a tithe to have the privilege of attending these events.

Thousands of young humans scream and idolize performers, where some rock-star/s is or are jumping around on the stage, dressed in strange garb . . . as they try to make what they consider to be music; and, the response to these sounds by audiences, can only be described as worship. When we behave in the same manner at corporate worship, this is totally unacceptable! Here is something to think about seriously! We are worshiping that to which we ascribe ultimate value; an object, a hobby, or a person. Performers on stage that evoke the *flicking of a bic*, or the *waving of cell phones*, are actually being worshiped, yet no fan would admit that they are worshiping the performer. If the word worship is too strong a term, then perhaps the term idolizing the performer could be used. The heathens worship idols. We know, without question, this is a sin! Watch the younger generation at one of their so-called concerts, as they shout and raise their arms and hands in awe at the mainliner. Whoever and whatever consumes the individual so much, that God is not given the rightful service do Him, is falling right into satan's hands. This leads to the worship of the creation or creature more than the worship of the Creator. **Romans 1:25** *"Who changed the truth of God into a lie, and worshipped and served the creature more than the Creator, who is blessed for ever. Amen."* KJV

The Bible teaches us that God alone is worthy of our worship. True worship is our response to the ***holiness of God,*** and therefore should be **respectful** and **reverent**! If one's worship does not display respect and reverence towards God, but instead displays the actions similar to those at concerts, then worship becomes a show, and is self directed. This promotes exhilaration: and this borders on self worship!

TRUTH VS. LIES

In **John 18:38** we hear Pilate asking Jesus, *"What is Truth?"* Evidently Pilate didn't understand when Jesus said: *"Every one that is of the truth, hears my voice. Jesus is the Way and Truth and the Life".* **John 14:6**

We often hear "Don't confuse me with the facts." *We are down on what we are not up on* is more than a clever saying. The fact is: we like the statements with which we agree, and dislike that with which we disagree or don't understand. There are some who will always ignore the truth. We have heard this before "The truth hurts."

From our viewpoint, it is not an easy task to accept something new. So it is time to take a good look at the father of lies: that old serpent in the Garden of Eden. The serpent, being the most subtle (crafty) beast of the field, is used here because this is satan's nature. Look at this next passage of Scripture.

Genesis 3:2-5 *"The woman said to the serpent, "We may eat fruit from the trees in the garden, 3 but God did say, "You must not eat fruit from the tree that is in the middle of the garden, and you must not touch it, or you will die." 4 "You will not surely die," the serpent said to the woman. 5 "For God knows that when you eat of it your eyes will be opened, and you will be like God, knowing good and evil."* NIV

This marks the beginning of lying! satan the devil is lying!

Genesis 3:6-7 *"When the woman saw that the fruit of the tree was good for food and pleasing to the eye, and also desirable for gaining wisdom, she took some and ate it. She also gave some to her husband, who was with her, and he ate it. 7 Then the eyes of both of them were opened, and they realized they were naked; so they sewed fig leaves together and made coverings for themselves."* NIV

Now the trouble begins, because Man (mankind-men and women, along with children) can tell lies just like satan does. Now we know good and evil. So what is truth? Truth is **ALL** that is within the will of God. God does not and cannot lie! The 9th commandment tells us

"Thou shalt not bear false witness against thy neighbor." **(Exodus 20:16)** KJV

However, we are all masters at telling half truths. It is so easy, as the people of God, to speak and act in half truths . . . perhaps even a quarter portion of truth. Bible professor Dr. Bob Smith, told his students: "There is no such thing as a little white lie."

It is sad but true, that many churches have turned the truth of God into a lie. This common practice happens whenever we skirt around the whole truth of God at worship services, at weddings and at funerals. We enjoy making individuals feel good by not telling them the whole truth, and we call this tact. A little white lie seems so appealing, and they possibly get us out of trouble sometimes. Admittedly, there are those situations where we don't tell the *whole* truth. Perhaps the old adage is true after all . . . "If you can't say something good about a person or situation, then say nothing at all." The forbidden fruit is so tempting, but at the same time, we want our own way and still keep the peace. We don't have to tell the whole story! Unlike the famous broadcaster Paul Harvey, some pastors, and laypersons do not want to tell "the rest of the story." But when it comes to telling the truth about God's word, we better be faithful.

Pastors are quite adept at being tactful in this manner, I know from experience. It is so easy to skirt around the harsh and hard portions of the Word of God. One pastor, who shall remain nameless, bragged that he had never mentioned the word **'sin'** in a sermon. Some pastors never talk about the judgment of God, or talk about hell. Some subjects of Scripture are left untouched.

In our day, we not only tend to glorify lies: we amplify lies. Listen to television commercials, and for that matter take note of the entire media industry. Advertising rates very high on the scale of lying. Perhaps *white lies* are the most dangerous form of all lies. *Try it, you might like it* . . . is the suggestion of that subtle, tricky, lying satan! Before realizing it . . . the person is hooked! Lying is an addiction! And know this . . . we are all addicted to something!

This is a good place to mention that being truthful, involves more than the acceptance of a few Scriptures to match our life style (proof texts). Jesus is the *Way*, the *Truth*, and the *Life.* Following Jesus as our Lord and Savior entails much more that than memorizing passages so we can quote from the Scripture. Ponder over what Jesus Himself says in **Matthew 21:21-23** *"Not everyone who says to me, 'Lord, Lord,' will enter the kingdom of heaven, but only he who does the will of my Father who is in heaven. 22 Many will say to me on that day, 'Lord, Lord, did we not prophesy in your name, and in your name drive out demons and perform many miracles?' 23 Then I will tell them plainly, 'I never knew you. Away from me, you evildoers!'"* NIV

The words that follow are really enlightening, because many pastors and church members believe God exists, but this is not the whole story! It should be *humbling and enlightening* for all persons to learn that even the devil and his angels (demons) believe in God. **James 2:19** *"You believe that there is one God. Good! Even the demons believe that—and shudder."* NIV

If the devils believe in God, then what is so different from our proclamation that we believe in God? Salvation is a gift, so take it and relax. If the devil refuses to obey God, and to receive the gift of God's salvation . . . that is the devil's problem. satan thinks he is all powerful. He even offered Jesus the whole world, if He would just bow down and worship him. **(Matthew 4:8)**

We have to make a choice, even as the Israelites had to do at the foot of Mt. Sinai. **Joshua 14:15** reads: *"And if it seem evil unto you to serve the LORD, choose you this day whom ye will serve; whether the gods which your fathers served that were on the other side of the flood, or the gods of the Amorites, in whose land ye dwell: but as for me and my house, we will serve the LORD."*

We must take God's gift of salvation on His terms! We can't tell God what to do! We cannot tell God what He is like! We do know for sure that God is Holy! God does His own good pleasure, even when we don't understand!

Ephesians 2:8-10 *"For it is by grace you have been saved, through faith—and this not from yourselves, it is the gift of God—9 not by works, so that no one can boast. 10 For we are God's workmanship, created in Christ Jesus to do good works, which God prepared in advance for us to do."* NIV

God expects "good works" from Christians. We all agree that we are justified by faith through the grace of God, but there is one easily remembered Scripture for us to grasp and put into action: **Micah 6:8** *"He (God) has showed you, O man, what is good. And what does the LORD require of you? To act justly and to love mercy and to walk humbly with your God."* NIV

God requires more from us than the acceptance of Biblical truths, as though we have gotten ourselves an insurance policy for salvation through such acceptance. We say we believe, so everything is ok now: I'm ok, and you're ok. Good works and faith are inseparable <u>if one's faith is real</u>! **James 2:18** *"Yes, a man may say, Thou hast faith, and I have works: shew me thy faith without thy works, and I will shew thee my faith by my works."* As a matter of fact, we were created to do good works. Read **Ephesians 2:10** again (above). Love is the key as seen in the following verses.

Deut 11:22 *"Carefully observe all these commands I am giving you to follow—to love the LORD your God, to walk in all His ways and to hold fast to him."* NIV

Matt 22:35-40 *"One of them (of the Sadducees and Pharisees), an expert in the law, tested Him (Jesus) with this question: 36 'Teacher, which is the greatest commandment in the Law?' 37 Jesus replied: 'Love the Lord your God with all your heart and with all your soul and with all your mind.' 38 This is the first and greatest commandment. 39 And the second is like it: 'Love your neighbor as yourself.' 40 All the Law and the Prophets hang on these two commandments.'"* NIV

Galatians 5:14 *"The entire law is summed up in a single command: "Love your neighbor as yourself."* NIV

Love is much more than a sentimental feeling toward the Lord or another person whom we know. The word *love* involves participation and action, mercy, and helpfulness toward the causes and needs in our midst. We so easily tell someone "I am praying for you." Sometimes we need to be reminded that the greatest prayers come out of our fingers, and not our mouths. Talk is cheap: true love demands action from us!

OUR PASSIONS

As we grow to maturity from childhood, we are influenced by many experiences . . . those that enter the eye and ear gate, along with the many unplanned and unexpected events. Some of these events are life changing, yet at the time, we didn't feel we were doing anything wrong, damaging, or that would become permanent in our lives. In ones youthful innocent stage, the father of lies is always present, seeking to get our attention! Our conscience may say: "Stay away from something or someone . . . do not do this or that." However, as from the beginning, the serpent representing satan, keeps telling us "It isn't wrong, there will be no lasting consequences if you yield to a specific temptation just once." Just as it was for Adam and Eve, we are forever yet at our beginning! We are always *becoming,* and what we are now is what we have become up to now. It doesn't stop at this moment however, because what we are now, is subject to more change as our lives continue. The fact is we are always tempted to *compromise ourselves* so we may be popular and well liked by others. Remember, we are, at any age, still under construction.

We all need to ask, "What are my passions, i.e., where is my heart?" It has been said that our passions are what we worship. For example: If sports are our passion, does this suggest that we are worshiping sports? If cars are our passion, does this mean we worship cars? If music is our passion, does this men we worship music? Let us hope not! We all have passions of one sort or another, and this is ok . . . IF, such passions do not keep us from the true worship and service of the Lord our God, on a daily and regular basis. God comes first! One should never allow passions to corrupt our worship of God. We must remember that our treasures, or passions, must be kept in proper perspective. God is **number ONE,** and some day, not known to us at this time, all our passions must be left behind as useless!

Matthew 6:19-21 *"Lay not up for yourselves treasures upon earth, where moth and rust doth corrupt, and where thieves break through and steal: 20 But lay up for yourselves treasures in heaven, where neither moth nor rust doth corrupt, and where thieves do not break through nor steal: 21 For where your treasure is, there will your heart be also."* KJV (This is truth)

You may also turn this around to read, "Where your heart is, there will your treasure be also." We support our passions, for this very reason. As William Shakespeare has already said: "To thyself be true." There is only one way to be true to yourself, and that is to faithfully use and follow the Roadmap of Life—The Holy Bible. (This is where to find truth . . . God is truth!)

Do you really want to go to heaven (be saved)? There is only one way . . . **Acts 4:12** *"Nor is there salvation in any other, for there is no other name (the Name of Jesus) under heaven given among men by which we must be saved."* NKJV

It must be noted: the word used in **Acts 4:12** is *must,* not **may** be saved. It is the dogmatic **must** be saved. We are not saved by any of the philosophies of men. We are not saved by **Gautama Buddha,** the founder of **Buddhism,** or **Mohammed** the founder of **Islam,** (Mohammedanism, is the fastest growing religion in the world) and is the largest world religion. **Hinduism** exists without a founder, but is a combination of thousands of religions in India and is the third largest religion in the world. **Sikhism's** founder was the **Guru Nanak.** None of these man-made philosophies and teachings can save us. These leaders of world religions are all in their graves. Only Christianity has a risen living Savior! There is no one else to whom we may turn for our salvation. If Christ is not our Truth and Savior, then we are to be most pitied, since there is no other means of salvation. We certainly cannot save ourselves! And by the way . . . Christianity is not a religion . . . it isn't even at the top of the list of world religions. Christianity is a way of life—Christ's way. I realize that in our universities the course on world religions lists Christianity amongst the religions of the world. However . . . **Christianity is not a religion** since it is **not man made**. Christianity does not grow out of any man-made philosophy or teaching. The founder of Christianity is God, through His Son Jesus Christ. <u>God did not send His Son to earth to establish another religion</u>! Repeating again: **Acts 4:12** *"Jesus is: The only name give under heaven whereby a person <u>must</u> be saved."*

Sometimes we may ask. Is there really a God of salvation for everyone who comes to Christ? Yes indeed! and there are too many who are willingly ignorant of this!

2 Peter 3:5 *"For this they willingly are ignorant of, that by the word of God the heavens were of old, and the earth standing out of the water and in the water: 6 Whereby the world that then was, being overflowed with water, perished: 7 But the heavens and the earth, which are now, by the same word are kept in store, reserved unto fire against the day of judgment and perdition of ungodly men. 8 But, beloved, be not ignorant of this one thing, that one day is with the Lord as a thousand years, and a thousand years as one day.* II **Peter 34:9** *"The Lord is not slack concerning his promise, as some men count slackness, but is longsuffering to us-ward, not willing that any should perish but that all should come to repentance."*

Just look around at the glories of nature and read **Psalm 19**. (See page 51) All creation gives testimony to God's love for each and every individual that has been born, and someday we will realize the truth of these words!

The old serpent (subtle and contriving as he is), has his hand upon the Church. He thinks he is winning the battle, but he has already been defeated . . . Christ is already the Victor. The resurrection of Christ is the unchangeable answer to the human situation we face today. We must get back to the **Way**, the *Truth* and the **Life,** i.e.—Jesus. This cannot be repeated too often: Repetition is the best tool for remembering.

SPIRITUAL MATURITY and CHURCH GROWTH

We need to see *"Church growth"* as a matter of *spiritual maturity,* i.e., worshipers need to make a real and vital contact with Christ. Instead of trying to make our church grow numerically, by creating exciting programs that attract persons to corporate worship, we had better seek to humble ourselves before God and turn to Biblical Worship, with an eye on the unsaved, needy persons who are all around us.

One vital, basic truth needs to be mentioned before going any further! We are fighting a losing battle, with all our attempts to reform and renew the Church, until mankind realizes what God intended, from the beginning, when marriage was instituted. God intended that through the family, His word would be made known and respected from one generation to another. Without the proper foundation, the storms of life will destroy what we seek to build, regardless of whatever else we may do. "From now on . . . God save us!"

Why do so many young people leave the church after their confirmation class has ended and they have been confirmed? Do we think confirmation will result in spiritual maturity? The same thing often happens following graduation. These seem to be two disconnecting points for young people. I think we are finally realizing that confirmation does not confirm anyone in the faith. It is only a starting point. An individual may be confirmed; but, confirmation is not a graduation ceremony from the church.

Please do not fall into the trap of thinking that the contemporary culture, technology, or mankind for that matter, is ever going to solve our spiritual growth and worship problems! We are looking in the wrong places for answers! This is part of the problem, but not the cause! The problem is ours, because we have misplaced our goals, priorities, trust, and values. We have placed our hopes for Church growth and spiritual maturity on something emphatically other than Jesus Christ, who is the same "yesterday, today and forever." We just cannot go it alone! **Hebrews 13:8** *"Jesus Christ the same yesterday, and today, and for ever."*

The answer is not to be found in changing technology, clichés, or any of the countless other activities done which we think appeal to persons whatever their age may be. We need to concentrate on individual needs! *"People Need the Lord:"* they need to *"Come to Jesus!"* Because we are all sinners in great need! **This is basic!**

How do we convince people they have needs? If you feel no need to repent, you will not repent. If you feel no need in your life for Christ now, you will never search the Scripture for truth. The very first reality we all must come to grips with is that **we all have needs**, and the *basic need is to find forgiveness for our sins*. We are great self justifiers as we go through life, in order to be able to live with ourselves. Yes . . . we are all sinners! Again: **Romans 3:23** informs us correctly: *"For all have sinned, and come short of the glory of God."* KJV

Where is this need met? **Matthew 6:33** speaks to this need: *" . . . seek ye first the kingdom of God, and his righteousness; and all these things shall be added unto you."* KJV

There is but one God of salvation, in order for us to get into heaven! Our goal is not to build people pleasing worship services, but to worship as the Bible instructs, i.e.—***Biblical Worship***. If we are faithful to God, and stand on that solid ground (Jesus the Rock), there will be hope once again, and life will return to our churches. The key is *'To know as much as we can about God, through Scripture, and then be faithful and obedient to Him.'* Being obedient to the Lord is good for us in every possible way! Then the world will see us for what we really are: God's people, different people, or even as Scripture puts it—we are a *peculiar* people.

Exodus 19:5 *"Now therefore, if ye will obey my voice indeed, and keep my covenant, then ye shall be a peculiar treasure unto me above all people: for all the earth is mine:"* KJV

Deuteronomy 14:2 *"For thou art an holy people unto the LORD thy God, and the LORD hath chosen thee to be a peculiar people unto himself, above all the nations that are upon the earth."* KJV

Deuteronomy 26:18 *"And the LORD hath avouched thee this day to be his peculiar people, as he hath promised thee, and that thou shouldest keep all his commandments;"* KJV

Titus 2:14 *"Who gave himself for us, that he might redeem us from all iniquity, and purify unto himself a peculiar people, zealous of good works."* KJV

1 Peter 2:9 *"But ye are a chosen generation, a royal priesthood, an holy nation, a peculiar people; that ye should shew forth the praises of him who hath called you out of darkness into his marvelous light:"* KJV

Ephesians 1:4 *"According as he hath chosen us in him before the foundation of the world, that we should be holy and without blame before him in love:"* KJV

2 Thessalonians 2:13 *"But we are bound to give thanks always to God for you, brethren beloved of the Lord, because God hath from the beginning chosen you to salvation through sanctification of the Spirit and belief of the truth:"* KJV

If we can understand that the growth of the Church is a matter of **Spiritual Maturity**, and not a matter of dreaming up ways to suit various personalities in the church, then the Church will begin to fulfill its **mission on earth**. The **Great Commission** given by Jesus is found in **Matthew 28:19-20** *"Go ye therefore, and teach all nations, baptizing them in the name of the Father, and of the Son, and of the Holy Ghost: 20 Teaching them to observe all things whatsoever I have commanded you: and, lo, I am with you always, even unto the end of the world. Amen."* KJV

We cannot afford the luxury any more of simply saying "I believe in God," and then do nothing about that belief. The Church will not grow as long as we insist on bringing the world and its ideologies into the church. Remember: again—We are in the world, but not of the world. The Church cannot fulfill its mission if we try to turn it into a popular club.

The problem in today's churches can be summed up like this—we are trying to fine tune our churches in order to make them attractive to the community. We are more concerned with getting new members than we are with a person's spiritual growth. When we inquire about a church that has aroused our interest, we ask, "What is the membership?" Should membership be our main concern? The church is not a club or lodge. The Church is **the body of Christ**!

Philippians 2:9 *"Wherefore God also hath highly exalted him, and given him a name which is above every name: 10 That at the name of Jesus every knee should bow, of things in heaven, and things in earth, and things under the earth; 11 And that every tongue should confess that Jesus Christ is Lord, to the glory of God the Father."*

Ephesians 2:20 *"Which he wrought in Christ, when he raised him from the dead, and set him at his own right hand in the heavenly places, 21 Far above all principality, and power, and might, and dominion, and every name that is named, not only in this world, but also in that which is to come 22 And hath put all things under his feet, and gave him to be the head over all things to the church, 23 Which is his body, the fullness of him that fills all in all."*

One starting contact point to assist in spiritual growth, is the music used at worship. Music reaches far deeper into one's soul than does the spoken word. Even film makers know this. One obstacle we have not learned to overcome, is to know and experience the kind of music that lifts one to the throne of God; or, at least as close as one can come to that experience in this life. satan knows perfectly well just how to sidetrack the individual, and get him or her on the wrong path. It has been said that "a person can be very sincere in everything he or she thinks and does in life, and at the same time be <u>sincerely wrong</u>." Anyone can be inspired by music, and be led into the experience of truly worshiping the Lord. Inspirational music does not evoke the swaying back and forth, with the uplifted hands, or the clapping to the rhythm. It speaks much deeper than that to the soul in need. Repeating: "Be still (God instructs) and know that I am God. (**Psalm 46:10**)

God tells us, in His Word, what He is like. How arrogant we have become to bring God down to our level of thinking. What we should experience in worship is all about God: not us! We should praise God the Lord, and King of Kings, out of the depth of our hearts. This brings a holy calmness and a profound joy. It is far from dull. It is motivating, and enables the individual to give up worldly ways, have a change of heart, and be still, and let God be a vital and real part of one's life.

Again . . . all that is written herein, is definitely not "**Age related.**" This would be a calculated 'cop-out.' Persons of age (the elderly) may offer wisdom and direction to a specific need. There is a problem here that immediately raises its head: Many young people do not have respect for the elderly. They toss aside most comments by the older people, saying "Oh, that is their generation: we know so much more (better) now. Times have changed." It is not a matter of age; it is a matter of having learned something from experience, and quite often this means 'wisdom.' Therefore . . . older adults have an important roll to play in getting young persons to listen to wisdom when it is present. Older individuals need to learn how to connect with the younger generation . . . as they are most precious. They need encouraging smiles and sympathetic understanding!

Yes, we do live in a changing world. But—truth is unchanged! **God does not change**. We are in deadening satanic error if we think our worship of the unchangeable God, continually needs to be updated to attract the modern world. <u>The Church would be much more attractive, if it stood for something unchangeable,</u> like: The solid rock of Jesus Christ. (**On Christ the Solid Rock I stand**). To view and hear this hymn, watch the '*You Tube*,' on line as it is sung in a contemporary mode. This as an example of inspirational music, regardless of how and by whom it is performed. Please carefully copy the following site into your browser. You will be inspired by what you will see and hear on this '*You Tube*' site:

h t t p : / / w w w . y o u t u b e . c o m / watch?v=OQgD_Wg9DG4

"Give of Your Best to the Master." Please carefully copy the following site into your browser. You will be inspired by what you will see and hear on this '*You Tube*' site:

**h t t p : / / w w w . y o u t u b e . c o m /
watch?v=xZHsxz4t_wM**

In our busy world and complicated lives, it is so easy to be so consumed, time wise, that we do not give of our best to the Master! We present our leftovers to God! If something else doesn't get on our schedule, and we have time, we may come to a Bible study, or to the church for a special meeting, or for corporate worship. We use volunteers for most all that is done in our churches, but, are they really prepared for the great task before them, whatever their calling. We are called of God, and this is an awesome calling! Are we ready? Good for you if you answer '*no,*' because then . . . in that frame of mind . . . you will see to it that you get ready, for this is a calling from God and not Man. Never forget that lives are at stake! satan never misses a trick, and neither should you when it comes to serving he Lord.

The Church is losing, or has lost its integrity. Many people no longer consider the church relevant to their needs. The Church is trying to do all things to please and attract everyone, and this does not work. It is past time that we get back to giving the people <u>what they need,</u> instead of <u>what they want</u>. Church doesn't exist to meet personal interests. The Church is the Body of Christ on earth: it is for individual repentance, confession, inspiration, spiritual growth, and finally one's being fitted for serving the Lord. The Church is not an entertainment parlor for individuals to join together to be entertained, married, or buried. When we enter the church building we must feel a sense of awe: "Wow, this is the Lord's House." The Lord has promised to be present when 2 or 3 (or more) are gathered in His Name: and He is! (**Matthew 18:20**)

Pastors are not ordained to be 'people pleasers,' 'good Joes,' or 'popular comedians.' The pastor is on call from the Lord, and not to be Rev. or Pastor Somebody with new ideas. The pastor is really God's spokesman! The pastor is the main *spoke of the wheel* to promote *spiritual maturity.*

Most pastors are graduates from a seminary. What are our seminaries teaching? Look at Jeremiah, for example, and read what God is saying about the ministers (priests) of his day . . . and perhaps to the pastors of our day: **Jeremiah 50:6** *"My people have been lost sheep; their shepherds have led them astray and caused them to roam on the mountains. They wandered over mountain and hill and forgot their own resting place."* NIV

Jeremiah 12:10 *"My pastors have destroyed my vineyard they have trodden my portion under foot, they have made my pleasant portion a desolate wilderness."* NIV

Jeremiah 23:2 *"Therefore thus saith the Lord God of Israel against the pastors that feed my people; 'Ye have scattered my flock, and driven them away, and have not visited them: behold I will visit upon you the evil of your doings,' says the Lord."* NIV

Is it possible that pastors are doing the same thing in our churches? Even if Jeremiah is speaking about someone else (perhaps the Pharisees and Priests), this does <u>not</u> let today's pastor's off the hook. What would Jeremiah say to us today?

We look at other churches outside the mainline denominations and they appear to be growing. They have huge programs to suit everyone's needs. But let us be honest, most smaller churches do not have the people-power, the finances, or the talent to do what large city churches are doing. Our pastor's can't all be television evangelists, nor should they try to imitate them! Does this mean since we cannot do as larger churches are doing, we cannot grow; or, if we could only do as they do we will grow? Of course not. Pastors, even today, are under God's scrutiny. The responsibility of a pastor is to lead and feed his flock (the Lord's flock), regardless of its size. Admittedly, sometimes we seem to be more interested in building programs, and denominational polity, than in <u>winning souls for Christ</u>.

Are pastors doing a better job if, while preaching, they don't need notes, and are always on the move, never standing behind the pulpit? We hear this statement quite often: "Our pastor doesn't even use any notes and he or she walks all around the church when preaching . . . he or she is a real people person even while preaching! We sure love our pastor!"

If the pastor's goal is to be popular and well liked, he or she will no doubt become one of those *beloved pastors* in the eyes of his congregation. Is this what the Lord's call is about . . . to *be a 'good Joe'?* Actually, the pastor is up front *not so much to be seen as heard!* Wondering around up front, the pastor may even be a distraction by his demeanor. It is difficult for a pastor to be humble enough, so the congregation will see Christ in and through him. We still need the pulpit ministry. The fact remains: Pastors are <u>not</u> called to be personalities up front, but to be faithful to the Lord, and feed the flock through the Word of God.

What has been written, may have 'stepped very hard on some toes,' but there comes a time when one must say, ***"I've/We've had enough!"*** At the same time, it must be said that I am not the judge of anything written herein, only God is. It is time to serve God, and not just talk about God.

I have always gotten much more out of a sermon when the minister stands behind the pulpit, even if he or she reads the sermon. Content is more important for inspiration than showmanship. The pulpit ministry makes it easier to concentrate on what is being said. It is a distraction to watch the pastor pace back and forth as the sermon is being delivered. You know exactly what I am saying. Please give this serious consideration.

What are the basic duties of a pastor?

(1.) To preach and teach God's Word in the sermon content and in their daily walk. The Pastor is God's prophet, and a prophet is <u>not</u> one who foretells the future, but one who <u>forth-tells</u> the truth and Word of God. There is little desire to get out of bed and go to the church of my choice for worship, if I don't hear

God's word expounded, and get my toes stepped on from time to time!

(2.) The pastor should be available to all persons in need. He is their a counselor.

(3.) To call on the sick, in hospitals and in the home. Remember when doctors made house calls? Our family physician had to drive 8 miles to come to our farm home. He charged us $8.00 (one dollar for each mile) for each call. Not that pastors should be paid for house calls, but, if a doctor, in past days, could find time for a house call when needed, pastors should find the time for house calls as well. If the congregation is too large for one pastor, then get someone to help with the pastoral duties.

(4.) To administer the sacraments of the church: Baptism, and Communion.

(5.) The pastor is to officiate at Weddings and Funerals.

(6.) To be the over all administrator of what goes on in the local church, but he or she cannot do <u>everything</u>. The 'Everything' part comes under the of Administrative Board, Committees, and volunteer members.

(7.) To guard the congregation from false teachers and false teaching.

There is no way to list all the pastoral duties, but these are the basics. One might say the pastor's job is never done. It is a 24 hour a day responsibility. When I look back at my ministry, I know I made many mistakes, but at the time I thought I was doing my best. If I were to live my ministry over, I know I would do things much differently! However we do not get this opportunity, and in heaven there will be no need for pastors (I think).

It is so easy to be <u>down</u> on what we are not <u>up on</u>, especially when it comes to Scripture. We all have our proof texts, and other passages to defend our ego and judgments. Are we always right? Example: What was the real sin of Sodom? **Ezekiel 16:49-50** *"Now this was the sin* *of your sister Sodom: She and her daughters were arrogant, overfed and unconcerned; <u>they did not help the poor and needy</u>. 50 They were haughty and did detestable things before me. Therefore I did away with them as you have seen.*"

Read it again: this was the sin of your sister Sodom: she (referring to Sodom) and her daughters were **arrogant (prideful)**, had **excess of food,** and lived in **prosperity and ease,** and **did not aid the poor and needy**. They were **haughty** and **self-righteous,** and did **abominable (detestable) things** before the Lord; therefore He destroyed them.

Do you see our country anywhere in these words? I hope so, because *we are doing the same things*! Let us never again be so narrow, so judgmental, as to say Sodom's sin was <u>only</u> homosexuality . . . that was **only** a part of their problem!

There are starving children (human beings) in Africa and everywhere in the world, but what are we doing about it? Very little comparatively speaking, because we are too busy with our own abominations! We spend millions to elect a president, and other millions on personal entertainment. It is like we are eating at a huge banquet, while a starving child is watching right beside us, and we do nothing. Personally, I can't eat a meal while a dog watches me with those eager eyes, without tossing him a morsel of what I have on my plate. We are the modern Sodom. Sorry, but this is food for thought at least! People are starving right now, and they do not have the luxury of waiting for food, while the powers that be wade through all the necessary red tape.

We are so easily caught up and consumed with our *right way-ness,* our *easy condemnations,* and *concerns* . . . that it becomes difficult to see the tree for the forest. We need to stop 'playing church,' and stand for something, before we find that we have fallen for everything, and end up under the judgment of God.

CONFUSION REIGNS

What time should our corporate worship be held? What kind of a service should it be: contemporary or traditional? Should a local church have both services? Should a church try to squeeze both services into one Sunday morning? Also, can we make room for Sunday School? And of course there are some congregations that hold worship services on Saturday night. How can we please everyone? Many churches have changed their worship times so often, and still have not found a time that satisfies everyone, so . . . confusion still reigns. Because of human nature, we have made our problems almost impossible to solve. If things don't go the way we like, then we will either go to another church, or get angry and never darken the door of the church again. Our churches are divided, and we aren't the slightest embarrassed over this fact. We just wring our hands in helplessness, and tolerate the errors of our ways. The Church has always had its divisions from the very beginning over such details as: How shall we take communion? Should we serve wine or grape juice at Holy Communion? How should we baptize? What think ye of Christ? Shall we have instruments in our worship or sing without accompaniment? And as was mentioned earlier, should our Sabbath be on Saturday or Sunday? What time on The Lord's Day, shall we worship the Lord our God? How shall our worship service be conducted?

Christianity is not about making individuals feel happy, liked and contented? Jesus is said *"Do not suppose that I have come to bring peace to the earth. I did not come to bring peace, but a sword.* Of course no one can please everyone. About as close as we can come to faithfulness to God, is to remember Isaiah's experience of seeing God's presence in the temple. We are in Church to worship God, Who is high and lifted up (Remember Isaiah's Call). This is but the first step in preparing for worship, and overcoming the confusion churches are facing these days. Repentance is not just a word, nor is it feeling sorry for our sin. It is a complete turn around from one's past life, to face Jesus the Savior, and to live for Him from that point. It takes the work of the Holy Spirit in a person to make this turn around possible. The Holy Spirit convicts us of sin, and this should be followed by one's determination and turn one's life around, and be committed to the will of God.

Then there is the confusion caused by persons outside the local church. Recently I saw a car that displayed the word "ATHEIST" on its license plate. We are faced with, and have to deal with, false doctrines. Hopefully we know what we believe, and are on the solid ground with Jesus, and are not sidetracked by what is going on all around us.

Mohammedanism is growing as fast as is the apostasy (the falling away) within our churches. Could it be that we are not standing on the Rock of Salvation? This is a valid threat! People are seekers; but, sad to say far too many are seeking or look in all the wrong places.

I Timothy 4:1-2 *"Now the Spirit speaketh expressly, that in the latter times some shall depart from the faith, giving heed to seducing spirits and doctrines of devils; Speaking lies in hypocrisy; having their conscience seared with a hot iron;"*

Harold Camping (President and founder of 'Family Radio', in Berkley, California) proclaimed, "The age of the Church is over. Christ is returning for judgment day on May 21, 2011."

We now know that Mr. Camping was in total error! His basic tenants were: **(1)** If you do not believe my words, you are unsaved! **(2)** There is no hell. **(3)** Everyone in our churches today are worshiping the devil. **(4)** No pastor is telling the truth. **(5)** All churches are serving and worshiping the devil. **(6)** Get out of the church, and do it now!

One pastor who called Harold's talk show, was dogmatically told to leave his church and stop worshiping satan. Harold continued "Get a job. You won't make as much money, but you will be saved."

Admittedly, from another point of view, it does look as though the age of the Church is over, but this is not really true! The Church just needs to get back on track! The Church needs another Reformation!

How well I recall my first experience with seminary in one of the Eastern states in the year 1950. The first class I attended was a course on New Testament. The professor stood before the class and said: "We no longer believe that Jesus was born in a manger in Bethlehem: He was born in his home town, and not of a virgin."

I didn't need that kind of liberalism and untruth; so I packed up my belongings; went to the office and told them I was not ready for seminary yet—got my refund—then I finished out that semester at a seminary in Iowa.

The Church in the world today, in the main, has lost the respect of people on the outside. The Church exists for much more than the conducting of weddings and funerals, and to supply opportunities for fellowship! We have lost accountability in the eyes of the world through out divisiveness, and our fears to take a stand on Christian or Biblical principals. Coupled with this is the need to **preach the Word from our pulpits**. We do not always practice what Scripture teaches. Remember—there is but one Church (the Body of Christ). We cannot afford to be a divided people in the eyes of the world.

In **Ephesians 4:5** we read: *"There is but one Lord, one faith (Church), and one baptism."*

If we are Presbyterian, United Methodist, Baptists, or whatever: we are non-the-less one Church, each doing its share, and doing what no individual body could accomplish alone.

In our stressful attempts to reach the people in the world, we have forgotten this one great lesson. <u>If we don't stand for something, we will fall for anything</u>. It is time for Church members to stand up for Jesus in their daily walk. The old Methodist Book of Discipline outlines it very well, for those of us who are Methodist. However, some of this has been changed, as we say 'to meet modern times.' Times may change . . . but God does not change. Truth does not change. Love, kindness, thoughtfulness, hospitality, along with Word of God, does not change. People are still the same (through the ages). Remember, our environment and technology has brought more changes than one can comprehend. Yet, in spite of all the technology we have at our disposal, people are still selfish individuals and think they are in full control of their lives.

More and more churches are dying and closing all around us. There are people . . . plenty to fill all the churches on the Lord's Day, but they are so busy, and the church does not seem to matter any more, to those outside the church. ***"Our consciences have been seared with a hot iron."*** **(I Timothy 4:2)**.

Yet, people can and do change, and hopefully many will come to Jesus, because all <u>people need the Lord</u>! The only change that really matters is that change which occurs when people accept Jesus Christ as their personal Lord and Savior. But . . . don't think this brings us that *bed of roses*, or the *pie in the sky*, we so want for ourselves, and for our family members and friends. We are still very much under construction! Christians have a Great Contractor—God! But sometimes we question the quality of His carpenters.

There are many seekers in our midst, but too many of these are seeking for answers in all the wrong places. These individuals are usually made up of people who find the Church inadequate to their needs, so when they are called upon by the Jehovah's Witnesses, or listen to some spiritualism sect, their interest is again aroused. Why did so many people follow Jim Jones? Why are Muslims spreading rapidly all around the world? This does not change the one fact of all life: **Acts 4:12** makes it perfectly clear . . . ***"Neither is their salvation in any other (make a list of all the others here if you want) for their is none other Name under heaven given among men, whereby we must (not may) be saved."***

Many proclaim their allegiances, by way of bumper stickers and license plates, to an endless array of loyalties which consume one's time and finances. The fact still remains, yet unrealized: satan knows how to keep us busy; too busy for Christ's Church. We offer to Christ our leftovers, which in reality means: "If I have the time, I will pray and attend Sunday corporate worship when I am free to do so. I go to church on Easter and at Christmas, and this is enough for me." There are endless leftovers, and these are an indication that we are under the false notion that we are our own bosses and we can make the right decisions on our own? (**Invictus?**) {See Page 8} We all know people who say they don't need the church. A few years ago now, someone asked me, "What has the church done for me?" I should have answered that with "What have you done for the Church?" Hindsight is often better than foresight.

What think ye of Christ, is the prime and old issue. What you think of Christ, determines what you do for *"the least of these My brethren."* (**Matthew 25:40**)

Ephesians 2:8-10 *"For by grace are ye saved through faith, and that not of yourselves; it is a gift of God: 9 Not of works, lest any man should boast. 10 For we are His workmanship, created in Christ Jesus unto good works, which God has before ordained that we should walk in them."* KJV

Matthew 5:16 *"Let your light so shine before men that they may see your good works, and glorify your Father which is in heaven."* KJV

Philippians 2:6 *"Who, being in very nature God, did not consider equality with God something to be used to his own advantage; 7 rather, he made himself nothing by taking the very nature of a servant, being made in human likeness. 8 And being found in appearance as a human being, he humbled himself by becoming obedient to death—9 Therefore God exalted him to the highest place and gave him the name that is above every name, 10 that at the name of Jesus every knee should bow, in heaven and on earth and under the earth, 11 and every tongue acknowledge that Jesus Christ is Lord, to the glory of God the Father."* NIV

FACILITIES USED TO PRAISE THE LORD

The churches build special buildings to assist in their ministry. But God has been out of the brick and mortar business since He tore the Temple veil. Yet people need a special place built to better equip them for serving the Lord. The places built for entertainment have certainly made use of the best of architects and very costly materials. We tend to gravitate toward the impressively large, beautiful and expensive places.

The best example of extravagance, in the extreme, is The Trinity Broadcasting Company, based in Costa Mesa, California; with studios and ever growing facilities in Miami and Orlando, Florida; Hendersonville, Tennessee; Gadsden, Alabama; Irving, Texas; Decatur, Georgia; Tulsa, Oklahoma; and New York City. Well meaning people send their dollars to support this sort of <u>extravagance and showmanship and call it ministry</u>. What we need to do, without apology, is to build respectable places of worship and inspiration that facilitate learning what the Bible teaches, and enables the proper worship of God, and at the same time witnesses that we are part of a unified body in Christ. As God blesses us with His presence, then we may call the place where we first encountered the Lord *"sacred."*

Communion with the living God is the essence of worship. Such worship is vital, touching the very core of our lives. **Perhaps this is why a whole book of the Bible is committed to worship ... <u>Leviticus</u>.** God commanded obedience from his people and at the same time was teaching them discipline. We are inclined to call all this *"Silly, difficult to understand, and outdated ritual,"* yet, for those Hebrews, chosen of God, rituals and laws were necessary to teach obedience. The overwhelming message of Leviticus is the **holiness of God. Leviticus 19:2 "Be holy because I, the Lord our God, am holy."** KJV

I realize many will say, *"But times have changed."* But; again, God has not changed. Are we really different people inside and out from those who lived way back in the time when Leviticus was written? Of course not: people have not changed! Only circumstances change. God has tried to make His will known from the very beginning after He created Adam and Eve. What God asks of our worship has not changed! Of course we don't bring goats, birds, and rams to the temple (Church) as a sacrifice unto the Lord, as was done in Old Testament times. The holiness of God has not changed, and our fear of the Lord is a healthy way to approach the One Who has given us life, and everything else we so easily call our own. Our worship of God must always be filled with reverence, respect, and appreciation for what God has given us. We are asked by God to live within the dictates of His commandments: and this is far better than sacrifices. From the beginning, God intended that He be worshiped as He directed: In spirit and in truth. Today it appears that we have reversed the process and we worship God as we desire, not as He desires. If you want proof, then look around and count the denominations, and the endless forms of worship.

In **I Samuel 15:22** we read: *"Samuel said, 'Does the Lord delight in burnt offerings and sacrifice as much is in obeying the voice of the Lord? to obey is better than sacrifice, and to heed is better than the fat of rams."* NIV

Proverbs 17:1 *"Better is a dry morsel and quietness, than an house full of sacrifices with strife."*

Hebrews 9:22-28 *"And almost* all *things are by* the *law purged with blood; and without* shedding *of blood is no remission.* 23 It was *therefore necessary* that the *patterns of things in* the *heavens* should be *purified* with *these; but* the heavenly *things themselves* with *better sacrifices than these.* 24 *For Christ is not entered into* the holy *places* made with *hands,* which are the *figures* of the *true; but into heaven itself, now* to *appear in the presence* of *God for us:* 25 *Nor* yet *that* he should *offer himself often, as* the high *priest entereth into* the holy *place every year with blood* of *others;* 26 For *then must he often* have *suffered since* the *foundation* of the *world: but now once in* the *end* of the *world* hath he *appeared to* put *away sin by* the *sacrifice* of *himself.* 27 *And as it* is *appointed* unto *men once to die, but after this the judgment:* 28 So *Christ* was *once offered to bear* the *sins* of *many;* and unto them that *look* for *him* shall he *appear* the second *time without sin* unto *unto salvation."*

Again: times have changed, but mankind hasn't. We have been the same sinners since Adam and Eve. It wasn't an apple, as artists have depicted it to be. We do not know exactly what the *forbidden fruit* was. We do know that Adam and Eve disobeyed God. God had warned them that the day they disobeyed Him (they ate of the forbidden fruit), this would be the day of their death; although the death referred to was yet many years into the future. But it did happen, and it is still happening! This was their sin and we have the same problem: we disobey God! We are selfish, greedy, confused, and unable to save ourselves: we just want to be in control of our own affairs! We will turn to God only when it is convenient, or when we have time, or in time of crises in our lives.

But God, none-the-less wants the same worship from us as from the beginning of time. God says: "Behave yourself . . . it is good for you, and sin is bad for you!" Calm down, humble yourself, and kneel before God in quiet humility; or, as **Psalms 46:10** continues to read: ***"Be still, and know that I am God; I will be exalted among the heathen, in the earth."***

One cannot worship God, doing just as he or she pleases. Consideration of others at worship is so important! Yes . . ."*They will know we are Christians by our love.*"

Words to "They Will Know We are Christians by Our Love"

We are one in the Spirit, we are one in the Lord
We are one in the Spirit, we are one in the Lord
And we pray that all **unity** may one day be **restored**
And they'll know we are Christians by our love, by our love
They will know we are Christians by our love.
We will work with each other, we will work side by side
We will work with each other, we will work side by side
And we'll guard each one's dignity and save each one's pride
And they'll know we are Christians by our love, by our love
They will know we are Christians by our love.
We will walk with each other, we will walk hand in hand
We will walk with each other, we will walk hand in hand
And together we'll spread the news that God is in our land

And they'll know we are Christians by our love, by our love
They will know we are Christians by our love.
And they'll know we are Christians by our love, by our love
They will know we are Christians by our love.

I Corinthians 13:1-13 *"If I speak in the tongues of men and of angels, but have not love, I am only a resounding gong or a clanging cymbal. 2 If I have the gift of prophecy and can fathom all mysteries and all knowledge, and if I have a faith that can move mountains, but have not love, I am nothing. 3 If I give all I possess to the poor and surrender my body to the flames, but have not love, I gain nothing. 4 Love is patient, love is kind. It does not envy, it does not boast, it is not proud. 5 It is not rude, it is not self-seeking, it is not easily angered, it keeps no record of wrongs. 6 Love does not delight in evil but rejoices with the truth. 7 It always protects, always trusts, always hopes, always perseveres. 8 Love never fails. But where there are prophecies, they will cease; where there are tongues, they will be stilled; where there is knowledge, it will pass away. 9 For we know in part and we prophesy in part, 10 but when perfection comes, the imperfect disappears. 11 When I was a child, I talked like a child, I thought like a child, I reasoned like a child. When I became a man, I put childish ways behind me. 12 Now we see but a poor reflection as in a mirror; then we shall see face to face. Now I know in part; then I shall know fully, even as I am fully known. 13 And now these three remain: faith, hope and love. But the greatest of these is love.* NIV

<u>DRESSING APPROPRIATELY FOR WORSHIP</u>

Because we have seen sign after sign on church bulletin boards that read "**Come as You Are**," it is advisable to make a few comments on why this has become so popular. Why are such signs displayed in the first place. These signs are displayed; but, for one reason . . . to encourage individuals to attend that particular church for worship, without going too much trouble getting ready. The implication made here, is that there is no need to get all dressed up for worship. You are welcome **just as you are**. What bulletin boards like this fail to say is this: no matter how you are dressed, you cannot avoid coming just as you are . . . a sinner.

This reminds me of the hymn, "Just as I am." Here are the words:

```
Just as I am, without one plea,
but that thy blood was shed for me,
and that thou bidst me come to thee,
O Lamb of God, I come, I come.

Just as I am, and waiting not
to rid my soul of one dark blot,
to thee whose blood can cleanse each spot,
O Lamb of God, I come, I come.
Just as I am, though tossed about
with many a conflict, many a doubt,
fightings and fears within, without,
O Lamb of God, I come, I come.

Just as I am, poor, wretched, blind;
sight, riches, healing of the mind,
yea, all I need in thee to find,
O Lamb of God, I come, I come.

Just as I am, thou wilt receive,
wilt welcome, pardon, cleanse, relieve;
because thy promise I believe,
O Lamb of God, I come, I come.
```

```
Just as I am, thy love unknown
hath broken every barrier down;
now, to be thine, yea thine alone,
O Lamb of God, I come, I come.
```

Indeed everyone needs to come to Jesus *just as he or she is* (a sinner)!

Dressing properly for worship makes the individual feel better about self. What is the proper dress for persons at worship? You are very special in God's sight. Please know that informal worship breeds laziness along with carelessness. It is so relaxing to have an haphazard and informal worship setting. You are present, and this is what counts, but is this the end of the story?

"Come on now . . . join us . . . Come dressed as is easiest for you, and whatever takes the least amount of effort. Come ready for whatever outing you may have planned for the remainder of the Lord's Day. Just come as you are!" Join the informal service we have put together to suit you, and your tastes. This is like saying, **"_Lord God, this what we are up to today_," so bless our efforts**! This is much too common an attitude! What we ought to be saying to the Lord is this: **"_God, what are you up to today_, may we feel the guidance of Your Holy Spirit to inspire, and motivate our lives for Your service!"**

The Bible does not say anything about how persons should dress when attending corporate worship in this **our** generation. This is good, because it gets us off the dress code bit.

The Apostle Paul gave very specific instructions to how women should dress in his day.

Two passages in the New Testament concern proper dress for women: The Apostle Paul writes in **I Timothy 2:9-10** *"Women are to dress modestly, with decency and propriety, not with braided hair or gold or pearls or expensive clothes, but come with good deeds, appropriate for women who profess to worship God."* NIV

In I **Peter 3:3-5** *"Your beauty should not come from outward adornment, such as braided hair and the wearing of gold jewelry and fine clothes. 4 Instead, it should be that of your inner self, the unfading beauty of a gentle and quiet spirit, which is of great worth in God's sight. 5 For this is the way the holy women of the past, who put their hope in God, used to make themselves beautiful."* NIV

When people gather for funerals and weddings, attendees dress in suit and tie, **most of the time** . . . this is the proper, and respectable way to dress when attending a wedding, or empathizing with the grieving family at a funeral. My question is this: Is God less important than a wedding or a funeral, so we may show up at His worship without proper clothing? God has given us the very air we breathe, and He has also revealed Himself in Scripture, and <u>in all of nature</u>. **Psalm 19** reminds us: *"The heavens declare the glory of God; and the firmament sheweth his handywork. 2 Day unto day uttereth speech, and night unto night sheweth knowledge. 3 There is no speech nor language, where their voice is not heard. 4 Their line is gone out through all the earth, and their words to the end of the world. In them hath he set a tabernacle for the sun, 5 Which is as a bridegroom coming out of his chamber, and rejoiceth as a strong man to run a race."* KJV

In this next passage of Scripture, there is a strong evidence that we need to be properly dressed, literally or figuratively speaking. **Properly dressed may simply mean '*be ready.*'**

Matthew 22:8-11: 8 *"Then saith he to his servants, The wedding is ready, but they which were bidden were not worthy. 9 Go ye therefore into the highways, and as many as ye shall find, bid to the marriage. 10 So those servants went out into the highways, and gathered together all as many as they found, both bad and good: and the wedding was furnished with guests. 11 And when the king came in to see the guests, he saw there a man which had not on a wedding garment: 12 And he saith unto him, Friend, how camest thou in hither <u>not having a wedding garment</u>? And he was speechless."* KJV

Scripture tells us that **Jesus is coming as the bridegroom for His Bride** (the Church) and only God knows when. No one can be dressed in the finest of clothing every moment of each day . . . our labor dictates how we should dress. However, THE LORD'S DAY is and should be special! If you think the above passage of Scripture has nothing to do with how we should dress for worship, then give this passage more thought: we are the bride of Christ. Then; so, dress in an honorable and respectable manner before God at all times, especially at corporate worship. You will feel better! Read **Matthew 22:1-12** for a sharper image! *"Jesus spoke to them again in parables, saying:* **2** *"The kingdom of heaven is like a king who prepared a wedding banquet for his son.* **3** *He sent his servants to those who had been invited to the banquet to tell them to come, but they refused to come.* **4** *"Then he sent some more servants and said, 'Tell those who have been invited that I have prepared my dinner: My oxen and fattened cattle have been butchered, and everything is ready. Come to the wedding banquet.'* **5** *"But they paid no attention and went off—one to his field, another to his business.* **6** *The rest seized his servants, mistreated them and killed them.* **7** *The king was enraged. He sent his army and destroyed those murderers and burned their city.* **8** *"Then he said to his servants, 'The wedding banquet is ready, but those I invited did not deserve to come.* **9** *Go to the street corners and invite to the banquet anyone you find.'* **10** *So the servants went out into the streets and gathered all the people they could find, both good and bad, and the wedding hall was filled with guests.* **11** *"But when the king came in to see the guests, he noticed a man there who was not wearing wedding clothes.* **12** *'Friend,' he asked, 'how did you get in here without wedding clothes?' The man was speechless."*

Jesus shed His blood on the cross for our sin. **John 3:16** applies right here: *"For God so loved the world, that he gave his only begotten Son, that whosoever believeth in him should not perish, but have everlasting life."* KJV

No matter where we are, and no matter how we may be dressed or undressed, Christ is going to come for his Bride: you and I, if we are a part of His Church.

Pray that you are never asleep when it comes to God's promises! Pray that the signs of the times, and the way others are going about their lives, has *not put the Church into a state of depression, indifference, a slothfulness.* Remember Elijah's experience that grew out of his state of depression. **I Kings 19:10** He (Elijah) in conversation with the Lord said, *"I have been very zealous for the LORD God Almighty. The Israelites have rejected your covenant, torn down your altars, and put your prophets to death with the sword. I am the only one left, and now they are trying to kill me too."*

After his pity party, Elijah was told to get back to work as a prophet of the Lord.

Humans need a day set aside for worship and rest, and to remember who we are . . . children of God, created in His image! Dress properly for the worship of the God, just as you dress properly for swimming, for work, for playing basketball, for auto racing, for weddings, or whatever else you may be doing. We have been brainwashed with this contemporary concept of the "Come as You Are" type of worship. You will feel better if you dress for worship. But remember, you are coming to worship as a sinner in need of God's grace.

APPLAUDING AT WORSHIP

Is it ever proper to applaud individuals at worship? The answer to this is a resounding YES! Example: At the 2010 New Year's Eve concert of the New York Philharmonic in New York City, Chinese Pianist Long Long played Tchaikovsky's Piano Concerto Number 1: a flawless performance indeed. The audience not only applauded, they also cheered, whistled, and stood in approval of this performance. When one considers the God given gift that enabled Long Long to play a monumental work, such as this is; without the music score, i.e., entirely from memory; this shouts to me . . . *"Man is created in the image of God."* The animal kingdom cannot do what human beings, created in the Image of God, can do and are doing. Therefore: applause and cheers in this case should truly mean . . . *"To God be the glory."* Had I been at this concert, my applause would be directed toward God, in appreciation for what He had made possible through Long Long. The achievements of mankind continue to give witness to the grace of God.

Many of the great composers wrote their music to the Glory of God! However, keep in mind that Long Long was performing at a concert hall, and not at a corporate worship service. For sure, the performer deserves credit for using his God given talents. Applaud the fact that humans can bless us richly with their God given talents.

Recently at our worship service, we had a family from Pella play their hand bells. It was a magnificent inspiration to everyone. We not only applauded, we stood in appreciation! How did I feel? I felt as though God had given each member of that family very special talent, and this is what I was applauding. No one could play as they did without the grace of God! We would have been greatly amiss had we not applauded! One 15 year old boy was playing at least 7 large hand bells at one end of the table. There were 8 other bell players as well. The congregation was awe stricken! We were worshiping the Lord God right along with those playing the bells.

There are many gifted and talented individuals in our churches, with special abilities given of God. They, in sharing their abilities at worship, deserve recognition for their blessings and talents, along with their dedication, and resolve to the disciplines necessary to give of their best to the Master. They, however, are part of our congregation, and when an individual or group from our church family takes part in the worship service this is not a program, but done to the glory of God. The following is an example of what I am trying to say. There have been times when our choir sang a special anthem in praise of God, and the people remained in quiet solitude: they did not applaud. Why?

They were experiencing a very special sacred moment, and did not want to loose it through the sound of applauding. So applauding should seldom be a part of our corporate worship, for this sound does act like an interruption, and often the inspiration achieved is lost. As our son used to tell his brother "Use your head."

When children are yet learning about worship, we need to compliment them with applause. When our youth share their talents at worship, they are old enough to realize that the best compliment possible would be silence. Then they know they have inspired the congregation and applause would only serve to break the sacredness of the moment. After all, they are 'up there' to inspire and are not seeking approval from the people at worship. As maturity arrives, worship leaders no longer need, or expect our approval since they are using their talents to praise the Lord. Applause is used at performances to show our approval to the entertainer. Hopefully our worship of the Lord is not a performance. When mature Christians use their God given talents to praise the Lord, we should respect their special abilities that are used to praise the Lord, remembering they are not seeking our praise or approval. No applause is necessary. Again: **The greatest approval one can give to another who has praised the Lord through his or her talent at corporate worship, is holy silence: this indicates that the special music has inspired the congregation, to the point where they just want to be still and know God.** Applause breaks the mood of inspiration while at worship.

WORTHY OF CONSIDERATION

Adrian Rogers (Conservative author and at one time the President of the Southern Baptist Convention) has written a book entitled. *"What To Do When You're Weary Of Worship."* What Adrian Rogers has written, has inspired this section of my writing! I have freely used his ideas, without copying his text. I have added much of my own thoughts as they blend into his material, along with Scripture!

He suggests that it is wise to take a look at Malachi. It's easy to find because it is the last book in the Old Testament. Sometimes Malachi is called a minor prophet (his book is only 4 chapters long). The content of his message (preaching) is far from minor! It is powerful. And it is not just a message for yesterday; it is a message for today. Malachi lived at the end of the dispensation, at the closing of an age. Much of what Malachi had to say to his day, he could say of our day as well.

Direct quotes from Pastor Rogers, are shown between these symbols { }. The rest of what is written here are my considerations inspired by his comments.

{God, speaking through Malachi speaks boldly against the priests of his day.}

Could it be possible: even to the pastors of today? This is what God is speaking through **Malachi 1:6** *"A son honors his father, and a servant his master. If I am a father, where is the honor due me? If I am a master, where is the respect due me? says the LORD Almighty. It is you, O priests, who show contempt for my name. But you ask, 'How have we shown contempt for your name?' 7 You place defiled food on my altar. But you ask, 'How have we defiled you?' By saying that the LORD's table is contemptible. 8 When you bring blind animals for sacrifice, is that not wrong? When you sacrifice crippled or diseased animals, is that not wrong? Try offering them to your governor! Would he be pleased with you? Would he accept you says the LORD Almighty. 9 Now implore God to be gracious to us. With such offerings from your hands, will he accept you?—says the LORD Almighty. 10 Oh, that one of you would shut the temple doors, so that you would not light useless fires on my altar! I am not pleased with you, says the LORD Almighty, and I will accept no offering from your hands."* NIV

Churches today are under the judgment of the Lord. Could it possibly be that we moderns despise the Name of God in the same or similar manner, and we are not even aware of it? How could that be, if this were the case? Could it be that we really don't know the God of Revelation, from where all our blessings and salvation is made possible?

{The priests of Malachi's day were so certain they knew all about God, and were obeying His laws.}

What does this have to do with our worship of God today? We know from experience, that in all age brackets there are individuals in today's world who feel, if they are honest about it, that many people do grow weary of all this church going. Not every church member attends corporate worship regularly. We know that not everyone likes to sing, and it seems as though the world is saying {"I am sick and tired of all this church stuff."}

I hope this is not the case with regular church attendees. Those who go to worship regularly are not as critical; yet, we all know there are some who just don't care for {church stuff}. We had a man in our California congregation (one of the Jones boys) who admitted that on Sunday morning he had to fight with himself to get out of bed and go to church. He related how it would be much easier to roll over and stay in bed. But then he added these words of wisdom: *"Once I get to church, I am so very glad I made it . . . I need to hear the Word of the Lord, and have fellowship with Christian friends."*

{It is enlightening to read what the Living Bible says in **Malachi 1:5** *"O Israel, lift your eyes to see what God is doing all around the world; then you will say: Truly, the Lord's great power goes far beyond our borders! 6 A son honors his father, a servant honors his master. I am your Father and Master, yet you don't honor me, O priests, but you <u>despise my name</u>."*} LBP

{Malachi is saying the priests turned up their noses at God, to do whatever they wished in life and at worship. Then they ask, **"Who despises the Lord God?" "Who us? Us?" "When did we despise Your Name?"**}

Those high minded priests could not imagine they were guilty of such a betrayal of God! Unlike the disciples at The Last Supper, when Jesus said one of his disciples would betray Him, and they all asked *"Lord is it I?"* **Matthew 26:20-22**. All pastors today should be humble enough to ask this same question about their faithfulness to God's service!

{God's reply to the priests,} and perhaps to the pastors of today: {You despise my Name when you offer polluted sacrifices on my alter.}

Whew! . . . that lets *us* off the hook, because we haven't offered God sacrifices since the crucifixion and resurrection of Jesus. We too are so prone to be argumentative, even toward God, so . . . be careful.

{The priests asked "When have we ever done a thing like that?"} That is, despise the name of God.

Many seminaries and pastors, are excellent self-justifiers, as were the priests of Malachi's day. But {*God tells those priests "**Every time you try to be popular, and be a well beloved priest, you tell the people just what they want to hear: to take the easy and nice way out."***}

Are today's pastors doing anything to Christ's Church in the world that could be a parallel to what God is saying to Malachi? Are we pastors trying to be popular by giving the people what they want to hear?

{The priests in Malachi's day were trying to be 'good Joes', i.e. popular and well beloved by all.}

Some pastors may argue, as did the priests of Malachi's day—"We don't despise God! We sincerely feel we love the Lord and are serving Him well." Without serious self examination a pastor may be robbing God of His glory by putting himself in the limelight. No doubt many pastors try to be popular, well thought of, and able to preach without notes: giving them freedom to wander all around while preaching. This putting of one's self in center stage may well be a distraction from the message. Much attention is then called to the messenger: how is the pastor dressed? Does the pastor look good? Is the pastor using notes? Does he have a pleasant voice? Perhaps the pastor is even saying to himself, "they love me, and I am idolized as the pastor of this congregation." The fact remains, the sermon (message) is not about the pastor . . . **it is really all about God**, not His spokesman. This is why churches need to use their pulpits! When at Worship, the individuals should remember Isaiah's call (See page 38).

Pastors do follow in one another's foot prints.

I Corinthians 3:5-15 *"What, therefore, is Apollos, and what is Paul? They are servants, through whom you believed, even to each as the Lord gave. 6 As for me, I planted; Apollos watered, but God was increasing. 7 Thus neither the planter nor the waterer is anything, but rather it's the increaser: God! 8 Now the planter and the waterer are unified, although each will receive his own reward according to his own labor. 9 For we are God's co-workers. You are God's field—God's building. 10 According to the grace of God which was given to me as a wise architect, I laid a foundation and another is building upon [it]. But let each look to how he is building upon [it], 11 for no one is able to lay another foundation besides the one which is being laid, which is Jesus Christ. 12 Now, if any one builds up gold, silver, precious stones, wood, hay, [or] straw upon the foundation, 13 the work of each will become apparent, for the day will show that by fire it is revealed, and the fire will test the work of each one, as to what quality it is. 14 If the work of someone remains which he has built up, he will receive a reward; 15 if the work of someone gets burned down, he will suffer loss, but he himself will be saved—yet as through fire!*

So make of it what you will. In the above setting it should mean **"Everything is about God . . . Yes . . . even Worship is all about God."** It is not about me, you, or the pastor. We cannot give too much glory to God! What do we have that is not a gift from God, with but one exception of course: our sin. So . . . everything but sin, is all about God! And God has taken care of that one through His Son Jesus Christ. Praise be to God, that He has done something about our sin!!! BUT BE CAREFUL THAT WE DO NOT TAKE UNTO OURELVES THE GLORY THAT IS DUE UNTO GOD! Pastors, and Lay persons, should humble themselves before God, knowing that 'It is All about God!' Just one time Moses (and that is all it takes), in the midst of the complaints of Israel, lost sight of to Whom Glory is due, and he as spokesman, at that event, did not glorify the Lord before his congregation. Because of this, Moses did not get to lead the children of Israel into the Promised Land.

Numbers 20:10 *And Moses and Aaron gathered the congregation together before the rock, and he said unto them, Hear now, ye rebels; must we fetch you water out of this rock? 11 And Moses lifted up his hand, and with his rod he smote the rock twice: and the water came out abundantly, and the congregation drank, and their beasts also. 12 And the LORD spake unto Moses and Aaron, Because ye believed me not, to sanctify me in the eyes of the children of Israel, therefore ye shall not bring this congregation into the land which I have given them."*

{No doubt more than a few individuals go to church Sunday after Sunday, as if they are doing God some kind of wild favor: and, they sit in church and read their bulletin, then look around to see who is missing, and at the same time can hardly wait for the service to be over and say: "Well, I've done my duty, but what a weariness it is." The thrill is gone, the excitement is gone, and the zest, the joy of serving our Lord is shoved aside by other concerns of the moment.} So, **"Can't we try something new?"**

{"I am tired, weary, and I really don't like all the singing, and the preaching and the crowds,"} The excuses are endless!

Maybe giving the people what they want in a more contemporary setting will bring people to church.

The BIG PROBLEM, is that we think of coming into the church on Sunday as *Going to Church.* We do a lot of things in the church building that are not corporate worship. There is a difference between going to church and going to worship. We go to church for a church dinner, or for a church meeting; for a wedding; for a funeral, i.e., we go to the church building. However when we go to the corporate worship service, we are "Going to *worship* the Lord," God alone is worth our total ALL . . . and if this is boring, something is seriously wrong with the individual's attitude while at worship: an attitude adjustment is needed! Just be clear about what we are doing: we are going to worship, not just going to the church facility for an event. The church is where corporate worship takes place. If we have to keep changing the time and type of service, and how we worship to suit various individuals with endless tastes and mannerisms, the church will be tossed to and fro by every whim and doctrine, and loose its light!

Ephesians 4:14 speaks to this issue: *"That we henceforth be no more children, tossed to and fro, and carried about with every win of doctrine, by the sleight of men and cunning craftiness, whereby they lie in wait to deceive."* KJV

Revelation 2:5 reads "Remember therefore from whence thou art fallen, and repent, and do the first works; or else I will come unto thee quickly, and will remove thy candlestick out of his place, except thou repent." KJV

If at church you are bored, let me say that you are in a dangerous predicament, if the **joy**, the **zest**, the **meaning**, and the **life** is gone out of one's worship experience.

{Far too many individuals are bored with church. We have all heard of persons who've been absent from the church for quite some time. When we see these persons, and tell them we have missed seeing them at worship: what is the all too common response? "Oh, I know we should be <u>in church</u> (notice they do not say *at worship*), but I have been so busy lately, and besides, when we do go, we like to visit around at different churches to see which one we like the best."}

The Church is not on the same par as the religions of the world. Forget about all the religions of the world: they have their basic problem, that being, all of their founders are in their graves. Christianity is not a religion: it is *the Way of Christ,* Who is alive, and not in a grave somewhere! This is what we celebrate on Easter, and every day of our lives on earth! It would be a grave mistake to think that Christ the Messiah came to establish another religion. Jesus had enough of this to deal with at his first coming, as did the Apostle Paul at Mars Hill. Jesus certainly did not come to start another religion!

AND NOW OUR RESPONSE

If you have read some, or most of what has been written, you may well say, "So what! We shall simply agree to disagree." Is there an answer to this attitude or dilemma? We find a concrete answer in the *Be-attitudes*. Jesus gives us a guide for behavior, to avoid problems in His Church. He does it in **Matthew 5:3-12**. These are The Beatitudes (meaning exalted happiness). *The beatitudes are the instructions for a happy and satisfying life.* As in many cases, we don't read the instructions when attempting to put something together. We can do it without any help. However, when a problem arises, then we get advice from whoever may be watching: "When all else fails we read the instructions." OK! In the Beatitudes, our Lord turns upside down what the world considers to be the way a life should be lived. Living according to this ROADMAP FOR LIFE, will change your life! We all need to read the instructions! (See the Beatitudes, page 73)

One vital, and basic truth, needs to be mentioned in closing. We are fighting a losing battle with all our attempts to reform and renew the Church, until mankind realizes what God intended from the beginning—when marriage was instituted. God ordained that through family life, His Word would be made known and respected from one generation to another. Without the proper foundation (**marriage, family, and home, as ordered by God**), the storms of life will destroy what we attempt to build through our endless church programs. Until we stand for that which is solid and unchangeable (**the Word of God**), we will fall for anything! *Life is not a game!* The Church can no longer afford the luxury of all its experimenting and constant attempts to be contemporary, up to date, and popular with the world! The Church is in the world, but not of the world. The Church is sacred (the body of Christ). God help us!

SUMMATION

There are three considerations that should be helpful while at worship:

(1) Never enter or leave the Sanctuary during prayer, reading of Scripture or when a solo or choir is singing; i.e., special music. Wait for a hymn or another part of the worship before entering the sanctuary. This is a common courtesy to those already at worship in the sanctuary.

(2) Instead of applauding during worship, a humble but sincere "Amen" is much more worshipful than the mood breaking sound of applause. The word "Amen" is a solemn declaration, of agreement and, unlike applause, does not break the spirit of inspiration. A soloist, choir, or other leaders would rather hear a scattered "Amen" from the congregation, than applause. Loosen up . . . never let bashfulness stop you from saying "Amen." Worship the Lord with uninhibited joyfulness.

(3) Keep the service alive and moving . . . do not drag the service. Sing with joy and jest or persons may go to sleep out of boredom. Never drag the hymns. ***Psalm 95:1 "Come, let us praise the Lord! Let us sing for joy to God,*** (to the God of our salvation) ***who protects us!"*** The Good News Translation GNT

The book of Ezekiel begins by describing the holiness of God that Israel had despised and ignored. As a result, God's presence departed from the temple, the city, and the people. The book ends with a detailed vision of the new temple; the new city and the new people—all demonstrating **Gods holiness**. The pressures of every day life may persuade us to focus on the here and now, and thus forget about God. That is why worship is so important. True worship takes our eyes off our current worries; gives us glimpse of God's holiness, and allows us to look toward His future kingdom. God's presence makes everything glorious and worship brings us into His presence. Amen.